ANOTHER CHANCE IN EDEN

R. Nikolas Macioci

With love and thanks to my brother, Michael, who has done so much to bring this book into existence.

ACKNOWLEDGMENTS

Grateful acknowledgement is made to the following publications in which some of these poems first appeared.

"Choking" *The Raven's Perch*

"The Interior of Disbelief" *Impostor: A Poetry Journal*

"The Drunk Room" *Ginosko Literary Journal*

"Temporary Seduction" *Ginosko Literary Journal*

"Unwanted" *Ginosko Literary Journal*

"A Tourist on Pike Street, Seattle, Washington" *Ginosko Literary Journal*

"Coins" *Ginosko Literary Journal*

"An Autumn Room" *Ginosko Literary Journal*

"A Shadowy Tale of Summer" *Ginosko Literary Journal*

"Elegance" *W-Poesis*

"The Organist" *Bombfire*

"Phantasmagoric Migration" *Bombfire*

"Dad Exposes My Heart Even Though He Is Dead" *The Raven's Perch*

"Undisclosed Desire During a Teacher's Meeting" *The Raven's Perch*

"Bet" *The Raven's Perch*

"Candy Stop" *The Raven's Perch*

"Ignoring Sunday at the Irish Pub" *The Raven's Perch*

"The Deceptive Kindness of Spring" *Straylight Literary Journal*

"Emily Dickinson Delineation" *Tipton Poetry Journal*

"Rita's Desires in a House of Denials" *The Raven's Perch*

Contents

PART ONE

I think I've discovered the secret of
Life—you just hang around until
you get used to it.

Charles M. Schulz

The art of life is to know how to enjoy
a little and to endure very much.

William Hazlitt

EXQUISITE SURFACES

The Angel's touch is gone, the holiday over.
Christmas tree bulbs burn like hot, multicolored,
field flowers. I linger at the living room window,

stare through the tree's reflection transposed
over street traffic. My mind drifts, and I recall
a childhood fascination with reflections.

Every year, when I was a kid, Mom removed
mirrors from the wall, lay them on the floor
to clean. I felt from the moment mirrors were

removed, eyes of a room were gone.
On my knees, I would peer into the largest mirror,
wanted to lift an arm, a leg, reach a hand

into the backward image. I felt on the edge of
another universe where the ceiling was a floor,
where I would have to raise my feet to step

over a doorway. Every year, I imagined entering
that mirrored scene where maybe my parents'
divorce would be reversed, where my dad's abuse

would disappear. As a kid, I counted on it being
possible. At this hour, the special holiday feeling
is crumpled like gift wrap, and I curse the past

because I didn't know how, or have the power,
to enter a world of opposites.

NO ONE EVER TAUGHT ME TO FISH

Mom and Dad pack beer cooler, bait, rods
and reels into the 1949 Dodge, head to
Big Walnut Creek. My eight-year-old body
slumps in the backseat, already weary
from a fishing trip I don't want to go on.
I feel as captured as bait on a hook.

We unload the car, traipse through woods
to the creek. When fishing, my parents insist
mostly on silence which is only broken
by occasional ratchet sounds or a bait can
kicked against a rock. My parents exude
patience, satisfied to wait for a surprise
to slip out of the water. It's as if they are
in another world, one in which I am in the
background, ready to skim a stone across water
which will grab their attention and cause them
to yell at me. Instead, I gather sticks, build
a small house for ants, invent a story
that will take me away from perpetual silence,
boredom of adding up hours and counting
grass blades along the creek bank.

RARITY OF THE ROCKING HORSE

Myrna Collins owns the What's New? antique shop
in German Village. She knows me by name because
I have purchased many pieces of furniture there.

One September afternoon a year ago, I stopped in
to purchase a banquet lamp. That's when I saw
the rocking horse. It was dapple gray, made of poplar
wood, and beautiful. I wanted it. Ever since
I'd read DH Lawrence's short story,
"The Rocking Horse Winner", I'd been fascinated
with the child's toy. I knew a little history
about the item. King Charles I had ridden one
when he was a boy, so had Socrates' sons.
I even remembered the saying attached to the toy:
"Do not confuse motion with progress."
Myrna wanted $5,000. I wrote a check, loaded
the rocking horse into my car, headed home.
She claimed it was an authentic antique.
I had my doubts, but, in any case, I was satisfied
to own a rocking horse, a plaything that had emerged
centuries ago.

I had an empty, spare room, placed the rocking horse
in the center like the showpiece deserved.
Myrna had given me cleaning instructions, too:
Use a damp cloth, a mild soap like Murphy's Oil Soap.
It didn't need cleaning yet. It needed my admiration
which it got plenty of in the following days.

Was it a whimsical acquisition? No.
Often, I open the door, unleash appreciation,
get high on its beauty. If it were a person, I'd hold it
in my arms, close my eyes, and watch the planets spin.

DISSOLVING THE BOND OF MARRIAGE

After mom's divorce from my abusive dad,
we packed suitcases into the trunk of her 1953,
maroon Mercury and headed to Florida, our
destination, Ocala.

On the second day of our trip, we sped along
State Road 40 until we entered the main entrance
to East Silver Springs Boulevard. At a food kiosk,
we grabbed Coney Island hot dogs and Cokes,
bought tickets to ride the glass bottom boat on
Silver River. I was twelve years old, excited
as a school boy free from class. Dressed in shorts
and sandals, I was ready for adventure.

On the boat, we sat on wooden benches.
Everything about the boat seemed normal except
for the glass bottom. Our tour guide pointed out
vents we passed over, one of which suddenly
dropped to thirty feet. We glided atop schools
of multicolored fish, rainbows with fins, and
more vents that dropped off to breathtaking depths.
The water, sapphire blue, was clear as the glass itself.

After the ride, Mom drove to Sun Plaza Motel
where she paid for a room with two single beds.
That night, as I fell asleep, I thought I heard alligators
growl outside the window, or was it memory
of dad snarling, waving a gun around in midair,
threatening to shoot if we didn't surrender
to his captivity?

CELLULOID PROMISES

I plucked down fifty cents at the ticket booth,
price of admission for a twelve-year-old
at a neighborhood theater in 1953.
Glancing to the side as I entered, a poster
advertising *War of the Worlds* guaranteed
a great science-fiction adventure.
Last month, I had cut out a color picture
of the green and black flying saucer
so prominent in the movie, printed
in *Look* magazine. The second feature,
Donovan's Brain, didn't entice me.

At the concession stand, I bought
a box of Milk Duds, took my seat, and stared
at the heavy, maroon stage curtain
that would soon open to previews, a short
subject, a cartoon, and the double feature.
Usually, I had a crazy hunger for romance
and musicals, but a good sci-fi movie
grabbed my attention, too. I loved
Astaire and Rogers' pictures wherein
their escapades popped off the screen
in black and white. Technicolor of the 40s,
however, looked hand-painted, further
underscored Hollywood fantasy of which
I wanted to be a part. I imagined being
discovered as incidentally as Lana Turner
in the drugstore, or that some magical person

as high up in the sky as God would arrange
for my screen test.

Meanwhile, curtains parted, and I began
my getaway from divorced parents and memories
of an abusive childhood, entered a world
where my deepest yearnings materialized
on the silver screen.

THE DRUNK ROOM

I climb the stairs with hunger,
bring my breakable boyhood to my dad.
I inch to the door of the room he rents
from his sister, Mary, fold down with
back against faded, flower wallpaper,
wait for him to rouse from an intoxicated
stupor. After more than an hour, his eyes
open halfway. I forebear the hug
I want to give. It would make him cringe.

He rolls naked to a sitting position,
mumbles about forgetting, points
a gun of disregard at me, belt replete
with usual bullets of inattention.
The movie he promised
begins in less than three hours.
My twelve-year-old mind knows
routine: We will catch a bus downtown
stop, at least once, at a beer joint.

He wobbles to his feet, dresses, asks
how Mom is. Their divorce final,
Mom and I prize freedom from his cruelty.

Four months in bed with rheumatic fever,
I watched daylight brighten windows,
nighttime descend.
I worried he, drunk, would whip me

out of bed as thoughtlessly as he might
snap a sapling from a woods.

In the theater, he slumps into a seat,
head lolls, face slackens
to a stream of snores. I fidget, disgusted
that he has slid away to oblivion, stare
at the screen without seeing the movie,
ache for the dad I have not yet acquired.

THE PROVINCE OF PATIENT PROMISES

It's mid-afternoon in December, cold
as an igloo's compressed snow.
My thirteen-year-old fist knocks on the back door
of the brick house where Dad rents a room
from his sister since his divorce from Mom.
Aunt Mary Simmons utters a begrudged greeting,
her flower-print dress straining at the seams,
ample breasts leading me from the kitchen
toward stairs to my dad's room.

He lay naked on the bed, sleeping off a bender.
I edge close to him, his breath, stale as a cheap hotel,
escapes in small puffs. His plan to take me
to the movies waylaid indefinitely. I slump down
against the wall, bored, feel small as an afterthought.
I wait, need the flickering glamour of the big screen.
I wait, tabulate details of the room: worn, brown carpet,
flowered wallpaper faded beyond a distinguishable rose
pattern, an ashtray crammed full of cigarette butts.
Brain calloused from holding onto hope for three hours,
I fan through sports magazines scattered on the floor
beside his bed. When he finally stirs, he blinks at me,
asks how long I've been there.

Our taxi drops us in front of the Ohio Theater.
I'm in awe of crystal chandeliers, burgundy carpet,
antique tables, guilted filigree in every direction.
We climb the grand staircase, take seats
in the highest balcony. In a short time, Dad sleeps,

lips pouting out explosions of hungover air.
On the screen, doors of a renovated barn open
to a surprise of snow, the cast singing "White Christmas."

We taxi home in silence. I hold my hands
in the warmth of my lap, thankful
everything fell into place before the night ended.

DAD TAKES ANOTHER DRINK

For twelve years, Mom surrendered to Dad's promise
of sobriety, a spurious assurance that detonated
her dreams. Crazy drunk, he would tip her
onto the mattress, vow to give up weekend binges.
As a kid, in my bedroom next to theirs, I heard
unimpassioned lovemaking, pledges to change.
Mom and I, drunk, too, on hope he would become
different, had made a net of our arms, waited for him
to fall to us from the tightrope of inebriation
into abstinence.

After filing for divorce three different times,
Mom finally followed through, and in 1953,
when I was twelve years old, we freed ourselves
from his drinking and abuse.

There was never a time when Dad showed me
affection. Once, he held my hand as
we entered a downtown theater
to see Walt Disney's *Dumbo*. For a second, it was as if
I were learning a new language from him,
language that conveyed caring, but he held my hand
only to keep me safe, not to show fondness.

After the movie, he held my hand again,
guided me toward the bus stop. I was six,
and his fingers felt cold as December,
uninfluenced by any emotion.

UNWANTED

Dad used to brag about the number of women
he'd straddled while still married to Mom.
My eight-year-old ears had heard this one day
while hanging around our confectionary
on Barthman Avenue. My dad never suspected
I understood the meaning of his language.
So young, I learned how sex ruins lives.
I vowed to keep my secret away from Mom.

At home, later that day, I lingered
in the kitchen, watching Mom steam green beans
in a pressure cooker. The idea of betrayal
seemed like another person slouched
at the table with me. In the living room,
Dad sprawled on the couch, a football game
flickering on TV. Booze breath permeated
the room. I could have awakened him,
but in his condition he would have given me
only imperfect attention, so I slid into a chair
opposite and watched him surface toward
sobriety.

What did he dream? Would he like to be
on another drunken fishing trip or in the backyard
pitching a softball to his uninterested son
who could never catch to Dad's satisfaction?

Next morning, Mom worked at the sink,
seemed to stare out the window more than usual,

as if inventing something pleasant to see.
I followed her around the house while she dusted.
I think I even wanted to dress like her, learn
rhythms of being a housewife, cook meals,
be responsible for holding a family together.
I carried the weight of what I knew on
hunched shoulders.

I wanted to return to days when Mom held me,
read stories, nursery rhymes, made me feel
miles away from despair. At eight, I'd already
had too many bad autumns, felt like a withering
leaf, a leaf tossed around by parental turbulence.
This is the story I will tell when asked about
the beginning of guilt.

DAD EXPOSES MY HEART EVEN THOUGH HE IS DEAD

His relatives promised not to tell me
when he died, yet they handed me the news
as if it were a lunch I didn't want to eat.
They poured the announcement into the phone
like water scalding my ear. Days afterward,
I dreamed death images of a man I disowned
decades earlier. Following my parents' divorce,
he moved to Berea, a suburb of Cleveland,
where he married his housekeeper. I visited him
only once, never saw him again while he was alive.
As a kid, I wanted him pummeled from the earth
to escape abuse.

I didn't attend the viewing or the funeral, but
I imagined myself hesitating to the coffin,
saw him nestled atop blue silk, cheeks padded,
lips stitched shut, eye sockets deep as lies,
hands immobile that had mauled my childhood.
As a boy, I wanted to mean more to him
than his belt would allow. From this day on,
his dead mouth will say nothing,
his words of love having gone elsewhere.

RECORD SHOP AS LIFE'S REMEDY

A mizzle of October rain dampens my face
as I amble from the 1955 Oldsmobile
to Harmony Record Shop on Rich Street,
several blocks from the center of downtown.
It's early dark, and the idea of adding LP
records to my motion-picture soundtrack
collection exhilarates me. It's a school night,
but I've finished grading papers, reward myself
with this small trip.

I'm acutely aware that four orange crates of records,
and additional purchases, compensate
for my solitary life and repressed desires.
While downtown, I'm tempted to cruise the area
for a hookup, but considering the risk, forgo the urge.

The shop smells musty because the owner deals
exclusively with used records, most of which
have probably been stored in basements.
I thumb through bin after bin looking for something
I can't name: music that will erase memories
of childhood abuse, music that will eliminate guilt
I still feel for my parents' divorce, music
to allay confusion about sexual identity,
music to heal Aunt Liz's Alzheimer's and
the constant disruption of my life
as caregiver? Is such music existent?
Can it be found within cardboard album covers?

I chose the soundtrack from *Windjammer*
because the sleeve picture of a merchant sailing
ship appeals, suggests escape. My other choice is
The Band Wagon, songs that will let me break away
from life's monotonous tedium.

I pay for my purchases, leave. Drizzle continues.
Downed leaves stick to my shoe soles
like pieces of the persistent past.

MOVIE CHILD

Russell theater never measured up
to the other neighborhood movie houses.
Its chipped-paint facade, stained and shabby
seats reminded me of a tired, well-worn
prostitute. I knew that word from overhearing Dad
talk about women he'd been with. Nevertheless,
every Saturday, Russell theater became refuge
from an abused life at home. Nine years old,
I trudged thirteen blocks on Barthman Avenue,
turned onto Parsons Avenue for half a block
until the broken-bulb marquee came into view.

The audience, comprised exclusively of kids,
controlled rowdiness to watch a feature-length horror
or science fiction film and the much-anticipated
Flash Gordon or Hopalong Cassidy serial.

Afterwards, I dreaded the trip home. It scared me
even as I hurried through a derelict, three-block
section where, at this late hour of 11:00 p.m.,
drunks often lay on the sidewalk like abandoned baggage.
Sometimes, I ran through that area, pumping arms
to go as fast as I could. I felt safer when I could
spot lights in the distance from my parents' confectionery.
They closed at midnight, would return to their apartment
above the store.

As I climbed fifteen iron steps to home, teeth on edge,
anticipating the possibility of dad's violence, I longed again
for the movie theater where images flickered across my face
like freedom from fear and the promise of an ultimate escape.

APPLICATION FOR MY FIRST TEACHING JOB, 1964

The ten-page tome lay on a cafeteria table
like a tarot card that would determine
my future as a teacher. Raymond Radcliffe,
superintendent of Douglas County Schools,
handed me a #2 yellow, Ticonderoga pencil,
told me to return to his office after I completed
the form. He was rigid and stubby, wore
an off-the-rack, out-of-date suit the drab color
of a brown, garden snail or a roof rat,
lapels too wide to be stylish. I, on the other hand,
sat straight as the pencil I held, decked
in a single-breasted, gray, ultra-skinny suit
with narrow lapels.

I flipped through pages of the Curriculum Vitae,
noted sections for a person's itemized list
of their entire education, publications,
accomplishments, notable projects, awards,
honors, achievements, and professional experiences.
The last page contained a list of questions
I didn't read until I reached that point.

Douglas County Schools did not have a good
reputation. Bordering on Columbus, Ohio,
Douglas, by comparison, seemed cliquish
and ultra-conservative.

I began to fill in the CV, finally arrived
at the last page and the first question:
"Why should we hire you as a teacher?"
More innocuous questions followed:
"Why do you want to be a teacher?
How will you manage challenges at work?"
It wasn't until I reached the last question
that my temper flared: "Have you ever slept
with anyone of the same sex?" I felt as if
someone had dropped a bomb in my brain.
I wanted to tear the paper in half,
throw it in Radcliffe's face. Instead, I scribbled
in the margin: " This is too cheap a heaven.

I wish I were in hell!" I sprang from my chair,
ripped into the superintendent's office,
slammed the document down on his desk,
turned toward the doorway and, without
saying thank you or goodbye, threw
over my shoulder at his wide-eyed surprise,
"You know exactly what you can do with this job!"

UNDISCLOSED DESIRE DURING A TEACHER'S MEETING

He ambles through the library door, and
I can't look away from his face, handsome
as a model's from GQ magazine. He slides
onto a chair across the room from me.

The principal begins to speak, but
I'm not listening. I hear another language
on the tongue of my mind tell me
how attracted I am to this first-year teacher.
I try not to stare, look around at shelves
full of books, feel as old as worn bindings.

The principal introduces the new teacher, Joe,
fresh from college. Faces register skeptical
acceptance. I begin an internal dialogue with Joe:
"When you're older..." I nearly say aloud.
"When I was your age..." sounds even more
 ridiculous. "I'm nearly forty-seven, promised
myself I wouldn't get old." I shrug inwardly
at a mirror, him who has not, as yet, made eye contact.
Maybe he hates the sight of me throwing glances
at him. Maybe he's outraged I occasionally gawk.

The meeting draws to an end. Faculty sag out of chairs,
and I swallow final truth that I want to claim his beauty
for my own, that, in this unyielding waltz toward death,
I have a deep wish to be chosen by the young.

THE KID IN THE HUNGRY MASK

Hurt is refined in him, full blown alienation.
I sense this even before I retrieve his folder
from the student-records room. I don't often
consult records, but trying to rescue this student
from ghetto life, I wanted all the information
I could obtain. His other teachers have failed
to assess his genius, that he belongs in a school
for the gifted instead of being placed in the hall
for talking and inattention. I have moved
his desk next to mine, and, since then,
his behavior is exemplary.

Thumbing through pages of statistics,
strictly information without a heart,
his background becomes obvious in words
mostly not written. Jack Atkins,
born November 14, 1967, resides at 1208
Indianola Avenue, a street he never trusted
in a district of rampant delinquency.
He tolerates his mother's sluggish embrace,
minimal affection, distances from his father's
frequent abuse, fist to fist fighting.
After baseball Saturdays, he lingers
on the sandlot, starved for coach's attention.
He has the habit of tightening his jaw,
tighter than the shine on a shoe.

I close the folder, full of details about a life
harder than wood, stare at the wall, hoping

I can make a significant difference for
a misunderstood boy, his father's wrong child
carefully wounded.

A GIRL ON A GLARING SPRING DAY

I'm staying for a weekend at Aunt Ada's
cottage on Big Darby Creek. She will join me
in a day or two. For the moment, I am alone,
lounging in a webbed lawn chair on the porch,
lolling in May sunshine. Less than a hundred
feet in front of me, the creek glitters with light.
The sound of water swishing over rocks hypnotizes.
A girl, I assume to be in her twenties, and whom
I've never seen before, ambles out the door
of the cabin next to my aunt's. The girl shakes
her wet hair, apparently planning to let it dry
naturally. She is comely, in fact, stunning,
and I can't stop staring. She could double
for Zendaya, the heroine of Spider-Man.
Her flawless face smiles at me. I wave.
She bends her head down, brushes her hair upward,
straightens up, smiles again.   I want to call out
a greeting, but I'm daunted by her beauty and
am unduly diffident. Besides, language seems
too empty to communicate what I'm feeling,
and wrong words might reveal desire growing
in me like an emotional hunger. Instead,
I trudge inside where I'm safe from chance,
linger at the window, peer at the creek, thorn trees, sky,
as if shyness were my only option.

ALL-NIGHTER

Chemical odor of carpet cleaner
burns my nose as custodians run sweepers.
Other workers rush from one slot machine
to another, changing drop boxes.
It's 5:00 a.m., and I'm slouched in front of
Pink Diamond, playing the three-dollar max.
I arrived at 5:00 p.m. Exhaustion blurs
my eyes as if I've been driving all night
without a rest stop. Since I arrived,
I've hit four jackpots, have stuffed more
than five thousand dollars into my pocket.
Luck continues to let me win in small,
sporadic amounts. I feel as if I have
the casino to myself. Four other people,
early risers, play far away, so I am
essentially alone.

Like the genie from Aladdin's lamp,
a young man appears from nowhere, perches
next to me. I stare straight ahead because
I don't like to be disturbed when I'm gambling.
He asks under his breath how I'm doing?
I mumble okay. Before I can fully realize
what is happening, he presses his leg
against mine. A rush of fear floods my brain.
I pull away, and he does it again.
Without turning in his direction, I tell him
I'm not interested. He pulls his leg away
but stays seated. I figure he's followed me

for hours, knows I'm a winner. Fearful
but calm, I rise to leave, ask a security guard
to walk me to my car. As I depart,
I glance at the rear-view mirror.
The man is pulling out too. He trails me
almost home. I don't turn into my driveway
but divert back to the highway. He stays behind.
I drive fifteen miles from my house,
head toward the small village of Lithopolis
where I know the police station is, but it's dark,
uninhabited, has moved to a location of which
I'm not aware. He's still behind me. I turn back
to Main Street, and that's when he gives up,
disappears. It's dawn. Sun is rising, glints
off spring's new leaves. I exhale apprehension,
keep peeking in the mirror, lucky as
three red sevens not to have been robbed.

CHAIR

For years in the 1960s, I drove
thirty miles from Columbus, Ohio
to the Plain City auction house
every Friday night. I lived by myself
in German Village, a quaint community
in southern Columbus.

My apartment echoed from lack of furniture
I couldn't afford, so I grabbed bargains
at garage and basement sales as well
as at auctions. So far, I had an antique,
walnut bed with a headboard that almost
touched the ceiling and a banquet lamp
on a hand-me-down table.

The Plain City auction ran from 5:00 p.m.
until one or 2:00 a.m. Sometimes, people
straggled out as late as 3:00 a.m., loading
goods into their cars. I always tried
to arrive early to see what was going
to be auctioned.

This particular Friday, I spied a cherry,
captain's chair I wanted almost as much
as I wanted a healthy heart. I had to have it.
Around midnight, the chair came up for bidding.
After a headlong battle with one other customer,
I paid, toted the chair to my car, mindless
that I was driving a Karmann Ghia into which

the chair would not fit since it was almost as big
as the sports car itself.   Determination
outweighed impossibility. Somehow, I would
deliver this chair home on this very night.
Hoping the law would be lenient if I were caught,
I rolled down a window, hoisted the chair
with one arm, and carried it all the way home
outside the car window, gritting my teeth from pain
but happy and as satisfied as if I were popping a cork
on a champagne bottle.

COINS

I have never seen coins placed on the eyes
of the dead, but I heard it was once common
practice when corpses were kept in the house
for viewing. I imagine a relative reaching
into a pocket, fumbling to retrieve two
coins of the same size, unsatisfied
if a nickel and dime came out on the open palm.
I also heard that pennies were best because
of their perfect size and weight. Otherwise,
the shine of silver might mislead, suggest
the eyes had not seen death.

The snowy, February, Sunday afternoon
Uncle Toots died, I slumped on the edge
of his bed, my eyes locked to his
cataracts and their unalterable stare.
I stood up, searched pockets for change.
My pockets were empty, no jingle
or chink. His wife, Aunt Liz, sobbed
in the living room. She and I were the only two
in the house, so I felt compelled to close
his eyes. I spread two fingers, pulled his eyelids
down, darkening the dark. When I removed
my hand, the lids retracted a quarter of an inch
as if to tell me I must try again. I shut them
three more times until they stayed in place.

That afternoon, as snow blew in white gales
past bedroom windows and my uncle's body

lay stiffening, I closed the eyes of the dead
without fear, hesitation, or the old-fashioned
help of coins.

IGNORING SUNDAY AT THE IRISH PUB

Thump of Britney Spears' *Crazy* pounds rafters.
Fifteen gay people gab in groups.
The bartender sports a tanning-booth bronze,
hides eyes behind over-sized sunglasses.
Weather shifts as abruptly as a clicked-off
phone call. All fifteen people move
to the driest area of the patio, re-group, chatter
louder than the thunderous deluge.
An off-duty barmaid named Megan, stops
at my table, impressed when I tell her I'm a writer.
She flits through a brief conversation, invites me
to stop by when she's working.

Soon after, a nameless man, bejeweled in gold
bracelets, rings, necklace, launches into a diatribe
about two daughters, both unemployed teachers.
He throws me a hasty goodbye, bounces toward
the parking lot.

It's a little more crowded now. Rain, louder
than a drum circle, beats off a corrugated,
aluminum roof, drowns out human voices.

It's the first time I've been in a gay bar
in over a year. I came because I hate Sundays,
and this place obliterates that day with camaraderie
and ready friendship. The disenfranchised extend
easy welcomes.

Deafening rain continues, but a hint of incipient
sun beams across a string of rainbow banners,
increasing the chance for an actual rainbow.

TEMPORARY SEDUCTION

He's slouched on a bar stool,
wears a light blue Henley golf shirt,
Levi's. His feet, in brown loafers, titter
on lower railing of the stool. My best
friend, Sandy, wants to introduce me
after she finishes a retirement party,
appreciation speech. I'm across
from him, leaning against a wall, waiting.
He looks sporty . I feel overdressed
in suit, white shirt and necktie. Sandy
says follow me. We cross the room
to where Joe's hand grips a sweaty bottle
of Yuengling. During the handshake,
I pull away a little too fast because
I fear he will sense I want to hold it
longer. Inclination toward infatuation
surfaces. What I really desire
is to dance with my arms around him.
I imagine us lying down together, nested
in silence and mutual affection. I stop
fantasizing, ask questions to learn
surface facts, slide onto a stool,
continue chit chat. He's younger than I,
skin tanned and tight. I feel centuries old.
His brown eyes look tired. I'm wringing
figurative hands to determine if he cares
to continue the conversation. I'm also
floating a little from booze, can't decide
what to say next. I want to invite him home

so I can roll away years of solitude. Not
much left to say, I squeak out glad
to have met you and drift away,
heart filled with sweet melancholy.

EVERYTHING ABOUT A BRIEF INFATUATION

My windshield blurs with rain. I rush
to the entrance of Barnes & Noble, step inside,
glimpse the clerk sitting at the cashier's desk.
He is as striking as a young man in a toothpaste ad.
I saunter toward rows of books, but maintain
a view of him as I pretend to look for a title.

When a store consultant approaches, asks
if she can help, I stutter out a random title.
She returns to her desk, consults a directory
to see if the book exists. I follow, glance
at the young man whenever I can, chastise myself
for wanting instant romance with a stranger.
He has already become a poem in my head,
a psychological wound from wanting something
out of reach. Why am I always weakened
by another man's beauty? Why am I embarrassed
by my own fantasies?

The woman says the book is not available
in the store but can be ordered. I thank her,
say I'll think about it. I pick up a copy
of *Writer's Digest*, head to checkout. I wait
three customers from him, think about
the frozen human within me, frightened
of the moment we will come face to face.
He sports a Joe Burrow NFL jersey, short,
brown hair glazed with product.

"Did you find everything you're looking for?"
he asks. Irony of his question stuns me.
I squeak out yes. Do the thousands of lonely,
Friday nights flood like ghost hymns from my voice?
Surrendering to the death of imagination,
the same death we hear about every Sunday
in church, I focus on the transaction.
He thanks me for my purchase, and I turn
to leave, wonder if he has graded me
as my seventh-grade teacher did when I trembled
at the chalkboard, feverish and wanting
to spell "desert" and not "dessert" correctly.

LINEMAN

I step back into my house when I see
your boom-lift truck parked in your
driveway across the road.

I picture you standing on the elevated
work platform, wearing gloves, boots,
a hard hat, an insulated tool belt

containing voltmeters, voltage detector,
the quintessential image of many people's
sexual fantasy. I'm reluctant to trudge

to the mailbox when I know you're home.
Small talk would only underscore longing
for you, an affable, easy-going,

twenty-five-year-old guy barely removed
from adolescence. I'm an old man who must
keep adoration of and fondness for you

to himself. Sometimes, I peer through
a window, see you shirtless mowing the lawn,
wonder why I'm so enticed to want more.

I answer that it's only God clearing the way
for yet another dead-end desire. I manage
to avoid your open-face smile most of the time

which is not fair to the neighborly friendship
I think you want. I once saw you on your front
porch, tangled in the arms of the girl

who lives with you, imagined you both in bed
naked, felt an ice-watery chill ripple
down my chest, swallowed the shock of envy.

I want to stop my imagination from wanting
to possess you, to bury futility as deep in my mind
as I can, to move among daily tasks
without infatuation eating chunks of my heart.

BLUE SUNFISH

The blue sunfish anchors at Fairfield Beach.
Aboard, a sailor unbuttons his shirt, sprawls
on deck, sunbathing. With binoculars, I watch
him from shore. He stubs out a cigarette,
lies basking in the glittering air.

Farther out, a fisherman on a pontoon lounges
in a vinyl-covered chair, self-absorbed, oiled
arms, chest, a plastic radio beside a thin ankle.

On the sailboat, the young man twitches a fly
off a sleeping eyelid. I stand barefoot on sand.
Beside me, a tan swimmer thrashes from water,
whips a towel across his body, staggers down
to his knees and stretches out on the towel.

I'm surrounded by leisurely men who create
a tension of longing in me, a need to connect.

The boy on the sailboat rouses, lathers himself
with lotion, tacks until he's a dot on the horizon.
I lose him to distance. In fact, when I lift a hand
toward the lake, he fits on the tip of a finger.

I roll up my towel, adjust sunglasses
the lenses of which have a blue tint.
Maybe it wasn't a blue sailboat. Maybe,
sooner or later, everything ends up blue.

SUNFISH ON THE EDGE OF THE WORLD

The mainsail jabbers breeze along sail panels.
Batten pockets, silk ribs, billow against

cornflower blue sky. The centerboard slices water
as if to cut Buckeye Lake in half. I steer toward

the horizon, the farthest point from my known world.
Two sounds predominate: slosh of water against hull

and the emptiness of spatial silence. Occasionally,
a ring-billed gull glides into view, hovers above

the sunfish then flashes away like a sliver
of white-bellied light. I head into the sun which defeats

tinted glasses, my skin aflame with pinpoints of fire.
An outboard motorboat zooms past me. My sailboat

undulates over backwash, rising, falling, rising, falling
like lust. I feel no shame in my pleasure of that sensation,

the joy of shaping my limbs with carnal air. I am
surrounded by water, a temporary gift of escape,

wish I had a glass bottom boat in which, after dark,
I could watch the lake brim with stars.

AFTERMATH OF SATURDAY NIGHT

The snail-like morning empties it's fuzzy breath
down my throat. My skull is smeared with headache
and regret. Sun squeezes through Venetian blinds,

spotlights vomit of a hangover on the bathroom floor.
I step around it, affording reverence where I can,
do my best to clear sonar-like buzz from my ears.

My brain roars like a motorcycle engine or the
gut-angry growl of a lion. Eventually, the sound fades
a little, leaves behind a mechanical echo. I gaze

outside at Sunday morning. The sky bleeds blue,
a perfect wound. In the flower garden, zinnias double
over, multicolor humps slipping loose from stems.

I step away from the window, dismayed
that I did not kill the despairing child in me with liquor.
Memories of an abusive dad hover, haunt, and hang

like black webs in the back of my brain. He didn't care
if I had a birthday cake or a reprieve from his belt.
I lay a cold cloth on my forehead, flop on the bed,

dream of a dark closet in which he once locked me,
clothes bumping my head, half dropping from hangers.

ROUTINE SONG

Rain stammers windows in cold, November
streaks. My naked skin rids itself of clothes
like useless gifts. I lean back on the cat-soft
pillow of midnight, loosen from tight, sober
arguments of despair, drift into the smoke of
dreams. Black and red flowers bloom and
burst at the center of my brain.

Morning silence surrounds everything.
I spread margarine on toast, brew coffee,
remake the bed, search for meaningful words
in my mind that clarify existence. Alone
in this house, eventually I will roam
from room to room as if looking for
an imagined friend or lover, someone
who will glitter into being and bring
an embrace to flesh into which fangs
of loneliness have sunk, clamped its jaws
on jaded solitude.

BITTERSWEET

The cemetery gate squeaks open,
and I slouch toward my parents' graves.
My brother and I have not bought
a monument yet, probably never will.
We seem satisfied with the flat stone
furnished by The Department of Veterans
Affairs, given because my stepdad served
in the Korean War.

I perch on the wooden bench within sight
of the graves. It is two weeks before
the first day of autumn. Sky is an intense,
gentian blue. Leaves on the huge maple tree
on the hill beside me have turned into
thousands of yellow coins spent by
an occasional wisp of wind.
Sun casts a golden hue in the air.

Surrounded by tombstones, I think of
the inestimable pain suffered by those buried
here, a place where the trials of love finally
let them alone.

I climb the hill to the oldest part of the cemetery.
I can't read many of the dates time and weather
have obliterated from limestone. I find the oldest
marker for a person buried in 1809. Catherine G.
Bowman Richardson's monument appears to be
toppled, but on a closer look resembles an old-style

coffin. Shading my eyes, I look back toward
my parents' graves, can't see the marker
at this distance, can only see a glare of light.

I trudge to my car, take a last glance around,
meditate on the many bodies six feet underground,
each in its own box of eternal silence
in a place where there are no more promises.

PURCHASE

Benches bend from weight
of sweating bodies. People
have traveled to Plain City
Auction House to take a
peek at "What's doin'."
Bids fly by me
like momentary birds.
I rise up in the aisle,
my hand rippling air
for attention.
"Going once, going twice,
sold."
Why did I have to have
that hand-carved sailboat
I will be taking
down to the shore
alone?

A TOURIST ON PIKE STREET, SEATTLE, WASHINGTON

I roll your nipples between fingertips, a pickup
from the toughest part of the city. My palms
whisper over your nakedness, and you chill
like the moon or a suicide. Parting your legs,
I satisfy your hunger with my own. So far
from home, I'm sweating like an Ohio farm boy
heaving bales of hay into a loft. I want these
moments to be as intimate as in the movies,
but this twenty-minute scenario is happening
in a neighborhood where people don't ask
for romance. Subsequently, you dress,
rake money off the bureau, and leave.

Needing a pint of milk to pour over my late-night
habit of cereal, I walk to the nearest 7-Eleven.
On the way, I pass call girls, rent boys, hustlers
groomed with Brilliantine Pomade or Brylcreem.
One, reminiscent of young Sinatra, sweeps a hand
over slicked-back hair. Long-legged prostitutes
gaze at passing cars, beckon with their eyes.

I cross to the opposite side of the street,
avoiding two drunks slouched against a brick wall.
They pass a brown paper bag back and forth,
tip it up as if it were a secret elixir. This is
the same street where tomorrow night Miss Seattle's
float will drift by as if it were levitated, and she will
cradle a bouquet of long stem, red roses,
testament to her assumed virginity.

Leaving the 7-Eleven, I walk the last block to my hotel
a little faster, wishing I could rise on wings to my
room on the eleventh floor, safe as a hand in a pocket,
away from cigarette-littered sidewalks, shadows
that bend at car windows and lurk in doorways of night.

CHURCH STREET MARKET PLACE, BURLINGTON, VERMONT

A fountain spouts toward blueberry sky.
Gift shops, linked by brick, compound desire
for silver trinkets and figurines hammered
to sun brightness. Decaled ashtrays, T-shirts
logoed and lettered with all things of a moment
captivate attention. Tourists and locals pass
time in this commercial pasture, populate
congested sidewalks with smiling faces,
swinging arms, legs bending at knees to carry
them to the next thoroughfare, to the next
happiness purchased over a merchant's counter.
Maples line both sides of Church Street where
pigeons flap away from inadvertent pedestrians
and vendors peddle orchids, fish, caramels,
fragrant spices and perfumes. Sellers serve
the muttering and the silent under the shade
of awnings in this luminous, July oasis.

I stare at radiant sidewalks, light quivering
off shoppers' heads, silvering church spires
rising above rooftops in three directions.
I ask myself is religion really nonsense
in the end, the beauty of ritual a compensation
for unfulfilled lust? In front of a clothing store
window display, I linger with others,
focus to see through reflections the reach
of their urgency, their eyes maybe looking at mine.

HEALING HURT BY LETTING MYSELF BURN

The Atlantic sheds perpetual waves,
peels off reflections of sky. Barefoot,
I stroll Sanibel beach. Sun scalds
my naked shoulders. I stop, wade
into the water waist deep. When I rise
from crouching down to immerse myself,
waterdrops, like beads of blue cellophane,
roll from my body.

I trudge back to shore, continue to ramble,
feel as if I've reached the tip of the earth,
the edge of existence. An oyster shell lies
in my path, its pearl eye missing, it's inside
white as a bleached stone. I pick it up,
rinse it in the surf, an August souvenir,
empty as my life without you. I almost smile
at elegant failure of our unsustained romance.

I feel a kind of saintliness walking this shore
as if I've been anointed with a smear of God's
personal oil. It's after 3:00, p.m., but the day
seems nailed shut with insufferable heat and loss.
I continue to amble, alone as the island of Hashima,
take a deep breath. Stench of a drowned gull
drifts off the sun.

BAINBRIDGE, 1999

Route 56 South twists through fiery hills
of autumn. Fifteen years I've attended
the Bainbridge Festival of Leaves
during the third weekend in October,
seventy miles from Columbus.

Summer crumbled away like stale cookies,
supplanted by the occasional surprise
of a perfect day of sunlight and warmth.
Red-roofed barns blur by the window,
yellow of butter-colored sun melted over them.
I glance at red, gold, saffron shining off sugar
maples, flowering dogwoods, magnolia.
Sky, the hue of a Himalayan blue poppy,
slopes down to earth, disappears behind
dense woodland. In a farm field,
Holsteins chew grass, contented as monks.
Vultures scout for roadkill. Forests overflow
with rainbow tints, a gigantic,
court jester's sleeve covering trees.
I pass a tavern called "Good Earth Cafe."
Many motorcycles intimate a gang. I imagine
women inside wearing Tammy Wynette hair,
sashaying from man to man.

Cruising past the "Welcome to Bainbridge" sign,
I spot a Ferris wheel rising above conifers,
almost touching clouds in its cycle
to raise passengers away from daily routines,
lift them into bird-high escape beyond empty lives
and useless expectations.

DANDELION DIGGERS

Aunt Liz tugs on her thick, blue sweater,
follows me to the back door. I take her arm.
We descend cement steps to the sidewalk.
Threat of rain overshadows the April day,
precludes sun. She clutches a plastic
grocery bag. I wield a stick with two metal,
snake-like fangs on the end. Prodding
the green, lacy growth, I press the stick down,
pop loose the leafy nuisance, drop it into
the bag my aunt holds open. Age has
reduced her to this meager task.

I still see her younger, planting tomatoes,
hoeing garden rows, hacking sticky willy
away from the property line.

We continue around the yard until
the bag is full. When we return to the porch,
she asks me to help her up the steps.
I accommodate, a snapshot in the back
of my mind of her wearing a polka dot dress,
sipping a Budweiser beneath a metal umbrella
in her sister's yard. She was thirty-five then,
not eighty-nine, now, an almost toothless,
old woman, without children, she deems me
her sole inheritor. I have lived with her
for thirty years, her rampant platitudes guiding
me to safety, blandishments belting me
into common sense.

We enter the kitchen, her crooked mouth smiles
when she sees ·hyacinths she has shortened
to fit the appropriate vase. She plops into
her recliner, seems to shrink away in the big chair.
I amble to the garage, drop the plastic bag
into the trash can, wrap imaginary arms around her
eventual disappearance into death's inevitability.

A LITTLE LESS CHRISTMAS, 1997

I stare at decorations put up three weeks ago.
The plastic, Wal- Mart tree sags a bit with age.
One set of lights dies while I'm in the bathroom
looking in the mirror at a bad haircut.
An artificial wreath, purchased in the 1970s
at Lazarus department store, hangs
on the kitchen wall, two spikes exposed
where sprigs of holly dropped off somewhere
between childhood and now A foot-high tree
made of pine cones sits on the coffee table,
topmost cone reglued several times.

Aunt Liz wears her old-woman's-body tonight,
sunk into the concavity of her recliner,
head plowed into a pillow dragged from the bed.
She fell asleep at 9:20 watching CNN's catalog
of holes desperate and insensitive
people have punched in the world.
I linger by her chair, think how
Alzheimer's has replaced joy.
The room is dark except for tree lights,
a pyramid of multicolors, beautiful despite
the missing string.

Nothing seems to matter at this moment
except the modicum of peace between
the two of us. I have lived with my aunt
for thirty years. I am her surrogate son,
have watched disease descend on her
like a black shroud.

I flop into a chair across from hers,
find comfort in what light there is
in spite of dead bulbs among the dark branches.

DEEP IN THE FEAR OF APRIL

Aunt Liz doses in her recliner,
having missed the 11:00 p.m. news.
I snap off the TV, stand beside her,
reluctant to awaken her from temporary
relief of Alzheimer's. Her face is puckered
as if a string had pulled all her features
into the sewn look of a corpse. I touch her
shoulder. She looks up at me like someone
who is only halfway back from having
disappeared.

She shuffles to the kitchen for a glass of water,
carries it to the bedroom. This is the hour
when I am free from caregiving. I hear her cough,
hope she isn't spitting blood from pulmonary fibrosis.
Coughing stops, and I am relieved not to feed her
ice chips to staunch blood flow.

I turn the TV on again, flop into her recliner.
Strictly Ballroom flashes from the screen.
I've seen it twice before, am uplifted by its music
and lively mood. Dancers perform the Paso Doble.
He is spangled in sweat, slides across rehearsal-hall
floor on one knee, sleek as joy.

I turn off the TV again, slouch back into the recliner,
the only illumination in the room streetlight
burning a path across worn, green carpet.
I think about the dance, how the partners whorled,

dazzled in their expertise. I believe Aunt Liz dreams
about a near-death dance, one in which
her partner outsteps any strategy for survival.

GERANIUM

Grandma Mohr wears a grasshopper-green apron,
pokes a finger into the plastic pot to tighten
dirt around a geranium start.

She dwells at a widow in a cottage on a canal
an eyeshot from Buckeye Lake. Two other cottages
flank either side of hers. Mr. Wineman, to the north,

wheezes out an asthmatic "Good morning"
as he plods along a path that runs in front
of all three places. She dawdles

on the screened-in porch, raises a hand
to block sunlight, waves at him. Outside,
she bends, knees brittle as dry, decaying leaves,

plucks crabgrass from her flower bed.
She makes no senseless movements.
At eighty-nine she wishes she could climb a ladder,

knows her daughters fear she will fall
tending to daily tasks. She remarks about
the moment when an ambulance will haul her

far from these flowers, when life will become graceless,
when she will become a permanent part of the soil
from which she will not awaken.

NAMING KINGDOMS OF THE YOUNG AND THE OLD

I see much I recall from childhood
as I travel to Buckeye Lake to celebrate
the Fourth of July at Aunt Betty's cottage.

When I was a kid, Mom and I made the trip
once a week to visit her parents who lived
in a cottage on a canal perpendicular
to the lake.

I pass woods that stream by the car window,
a continuous blur of green. Past railroad tracks,
I spot the site of a hotel grandpa managed
in the 1940s, replaced now by a vaulted mansion
with an indoor swimming pool. A few miles farther,
I glimpse a willow tree dominating a canal bank,
a jungle of undergrowth hiding land
my grandparents' home used to occupy.

I park off the highway where gravel grates
under tires like loose teeth. Mom and Aunt Liz
greet me with hugs. I tease them about wearing
bikinis into the lake. They laugh. Other guests
have spread blankets along the bank. I don't know
any of these relatives from Aunt Betty's second
marriage. Most of them are young, brown
from sun. Under exercised, self-conscious,
I don't take off my shirt and jump into the lake
to escape humidity. The young, muscular ones

stare at me as if I were wearing a sign that says
I've gained too much weight, that my unfirm face
droops like a melting mask.

I meander back to the middle-age group
who lounge on wicker chairs, comfortable
with short sentences and absence of flat stomachs.
I wonder if this group guesses I don't want to be
identified with them. I want to walk barefoot

on the dock, wear skimpy swim trunks, be sleek
as the inside of a shell, dive into the lake
away from my out-of-date body.

It is dark as God's hiding place, except
for a circle of moon, when I sit down on a bench
to watch fireworks. Red flares placed halfway
around the lake flame halos of light,
make the parameter look like a giant birthday cake.
Boats bob at anchor, decorated with strings
of garish bulbs. A burst of fireworks flowers
a bouquet, streaks down white as a waterfall.
I wait for the finale: a fiery flag ends sky's celebration.
Crowds of people stream along sidewalk that circles
the lake, beer cans in hand. White-haired aunts
gather me to their goodbyes.

I spark the engine, flip headlights on, slip away
from nothing on earth I have to love
but family whose wrinkled faces and flawless resignation
wait for sleep.

SPRING AS AN ITINERANT TAILOR

He dresses me in March breezes,
clothes that fit like a confirmation of life,
clothes I wear to validate the force
of incomprehensible feelings.

It's still cool outside. In fact, it's overcast
and cold as ice cream, except
for an occasional burst of sunshine.

Clouds are formal, white gloves
filled with fingers of gentle winds.
The tailor lingers in the yard, ankle deep
in early daffodils, slips me into

a transparent shirt that smells of grass
and pine. The shirt, silky as air, spreads
across my back. A sudden surprise of

sunlight runs off its golden seams.

THE DECEPTIVE KINDNESS OF SPRING

The short, rasping song of the tanager, delicate
as a religious calling, drifts to my ear.
It's questioning voice answers itself as if
cross examining existence of late, April snow.

I linger at a bedroom window, feel
an unaccountable, obscure sadness.
The room holds a walnut bed with floor
to ceiling backboard, a student lamp, dresser,
chest of drawers, desk, a six-shelf bookcase.
I would call the room ordinary, but it's not
because of a self-crime perpetrated in it.

As a teenager, I killed who I really am
to please parents, relatives, friends.
I was a shy boy without love, suffocated,
grappling with sexual identity. I made up
enough excuses not to date a girl
to fill a spacious pocket.

Now, it's spring again. I'm entirely alone
with no one sleeping beside me. I'm old,
rage to justify myself transmuted
into feeble acceptance.

Twilight comes in an instant. I sprawl naked
upon the bed, a pinned insect on exhibit.
Dim radiance streams from a lamp,

twenty-five watts of illumination
pouring like apology over a body
I finally call normal.

PHANTASMAGORIC MIGRATION

I praise the injured sweep of broken birds,
watch them ruined by winter. Do they ponder
God the way I do or simply go with echoing
wings to where they stumble onto stray warmth?
Somedays, reveries seem to color sky
bluer than blue, and birds slip from shadows
of their own lives into sovereign clouds
that have the same exact look as death.
I found myself talking to those fragile birds
just before they faded over and over into
the chocking heat of Brazil. The roof
of my mind remembers the downy heads
of those birds, their crazy eyes turning back
to fasten a final look on me.

Now, I am as alone as a snake's rattle,
and the best birds have cleared out of town,
clogged air with escape. Now that they
are as gone as an old mill, I resent
my urge to be rid of them. They've left
the dying ones behind to talk to themselves,
to bear with ease their wrecked lives.

Was it my roving imagination that loved
those birds, that strummed the wires
on which they waited for handfuls of sacred
bread? We were made to part when time
sung out the end, but daily I lust for the
feathery sound of their unfailing return.

MOONLIGHT NEEDS A LITTLE SYMPATHY

The moon's existence has become cliché,
I think as I loiter on my driveway
letting myself be sheathed in celestial brightness.
I wear milky illumination as if it were
a second skin or a garment laced with October chill.
Through oak limbs I stare at intermittent strips
of the orb's glare, wonder how many other people
at this moment are transfixed by moon's inexplicable
embrace that elicits memories of lost romance
and tatters of relationships that broke down
like old jalopies? The moon has taken a beating
from poets and the general public who swoon
in its supernatural pull, fail to acknowledge
that light from the dark rock is illusion.

I wish I could finally name why the moon beguiles,
why it's appearance precipitates a dramatic effect
on our lives as it is on mine right now.
I cannot explain the fascination or the way
it assassinates the heart. I can only join generations
who have worshiped it as if it were a voluptuous woman
or the convenient object of any kind of imaginary love.
I don't blame the moon for its magic. I blame myself
for succumbing to its apocryphal influence,
standing long enough on the driveway
to believe the moon is there only for me.

THE INTERIOR OF DISBELIEF

Sometimes I feel frail as a parakeet
struggling to stay on Christ's perch.
I have become my own Holy Ghost,
proprietor of half a belief in God,
not ample enough to balance frustration
of curiosity against satisfaction that
cheerless religion promises.

In early years, I reached for truth, drank
a thousand beers from a ceramic mug.
There was no doubt in my purpose to
obliterate the trinity, to struggle free
of something less real than a Teflon pan
or the cutlery that hung in a neat row
on a wooden rack. I asked why
I couldn't touch hands with God, why
eating the wafer, drinking the wine
brought me just so close to apprehending
secrets only the holy had the honor
of understanding. When I stopped drinking,
I listened to concertos, appreciated
ethereal lift away from the abyss
of questions that ate at me like a rampant
tumor. The music cradled my disbelief,
turned off useless inquiry and humbled me
with common sense.

Since then I've pulled away from the piety
of churches, made a habit of feeding bread

crumbs to birds, watching them scatter
into the sky without redemption
or a promise of heaven.

PART TWO

I am a lover without a lover. I am
lovely and lonely and I belong
deeply to myself.

Warsan Shire

Have enough courage to trust love one
more time and always one more time.

Maya Angelou

ANOTHER CHANCE IN EDEN

An additional apple shines in the garden,
its legendary danger polished by sun.

Naked, Adam points his finger, names
animals again: lions, bears, cats, birds.

The serpent lurks in the tree, unwinds
from a branch, points its head in Eve's direction.

Consumed with guiltless curiosity,
she accepts the fruit, doesn't take a bite.

She knows the outcome, does not question why
her arm burns with hesitation or why

sudden thunder underscores her choice.
Her innocence intact, dazzles with permanence.

Adam touches her hand, takes the apple,
throws it into a field where it's metaphysical

power withers. Simplicity of existence
preserved, the serpent's tongue flicks defeat.

They are in the paradise that was before,
a sinless garden where a man and a woman

no longer live on the edge of transgression,
a garden as blessed as breath.

THE JUNE OF MUCH LONGING

Aiden, forty-three, recently divorced,
strolls into The Bixby Club, a place
not as hard to get into as Berghain
in Berlin nor as infamous as Studio 54
in New York. Bixby spoils gentility
with superb service and gracious manners.

A waiter leads Aiden to a round table
covered with a white, linen tablecloth.
Aiden orders Pinot Noir. At the next table,
a youthful, but middle-age woman,
reminiscent of Lauren Bacall, also sips
a Burgundy wine. Drink loosens Aiden's
inhibitions, and before he orders steamed
mussels in white sauce, casts her a look
of intense interest. She smiles at him,
accepts his stare with additional smiles.
He slides from his chair, approaches her table.
It is a moment beyond imagination,
a split second when he thinks he has
finally caught on to how to make life magical.

She says, "Yes, well..," invites him to sit.
He transfers his drink to her table, apologizes
for staring, tells her how she interests him.
Their conversation resonates with unspoken
affinity for one another, each word seeming
to carry a subtext of mutual fascination.
They study each other's faces, become

a two-person neighborhood in which
ceiling light enhances their attractiveness.

Having fallen into each other's rhythm,
they will eventually share a bed tonight
because of carnal urgency hitting them both
in the gut like an electric prod.

A ROOM ON EARTH FOR A VIRGIN IN WINTER

You taste his tongue, swallow between kisses.
His arms encircle you like a cure for solitude.

More than fifty years you have saved yourself
for this infinite rapture, shed shelter of religious

mysticism to lie with a man on enthralled sheets.
Light from a nearby lamppost washes over

your lost virtue and your nakedness. You met James
in a bar, liked his voice, his easy invitation

to lay aside the frost of your life. Even though
you promised yourself you would never have sex

until marriage, ticking off each year's clock
finally punched a dent in stubborn resolution,

and you waded through scant reluctance
to a neighborhood tavern. You press your head

against his throat, wrap yourself around his heartbeat.
Is this the moment you should weep as he rises

from bed and leaves you with a sudden vacancy?
You hear shower water, pull the patchwork quilt

around your neck as if to hide his absence.
He leaves without a promise to return.

Lingering at a window, you watch his car disappear,
stare at the snowy street, ruined white turned to slush

under late-night wheel tracks.

THE HUSBAND DISAPPEARS FROM DELMONICO'S

After a dinner of porterhouse for two,
he says he's going to the restroom,
going to find a life sweet as a rose.
She winces. Her husband is as solid
as a hardwood floor. What kind of
gibberish is this? A rose!

They had reserved a table with the
intention of celebrating their thirty-fifth
anniversary. Now this! An unexpected
disruption that might ruin the evening.
He weighs in as a heavyweight of stability,
has always made her feel secure, loved
without limitations. Maybe he teased her
with an impulsive quip, an impetuous joke.

When too much time has passed for her
to remain comfortable with his absence,
she asks her waiter if he would be kind
enough to look in the restroom for a tall man
in a light gray suit. The waiter returns,
says there is no such man in there.
She panics, confused about what to do next,
rushes to the valet, fumbles the parking ticket
from her purse. The Mercedes slows to a stop
in front of her. She climbs in, heads toward
their penthouse on Sutton Place South.

He is neither there nor anywhere she checks
in the following months. A missing person's
report yields nothing. She remembers
in the 1970s, divorce rates soared,
people felt freer to leave marriages that were
abusive or unsatisfactory, but her relationship
sidestepped both characteristics.

Years accumulate, and she wears the conundrum
like an unexplainable coat of guilt, odor of roses
abhorrent, detestable as the night he broke loose
from their marriage without an explanation.

INSTALLING A SHORT BLOCK

A little after midnight, we begin,
sort necessary tools from the toolbox
onto the driveway. My friend, Tate,
and I loosen bolts, remove a defunct
short block from the Wheel Horse
lawn tractor, leave a black hole
as if we had excised a tumor. We place
the new engine into the empty space.
Tate strips wires, ready to hook them
to proper terminals. He and I lie parallel
on a canvas tarp, a bald work light near
our heads, hands stiff with April cold.
I am warmed only by thoughts of my
desire for him. He is married, but
we have nursed a platonic relationship
for several years. I want more. Working
in this intimate situation is the closest
I will ever get to a consummation.
He finishes the last connection, says
"I guess that's it," stands, stretches, arches
his back, asks if we should start it.
I guess I don't have to tell him yes because
he sniffs once, turns the key. Like the roar
of a rig on a distant highway sound vrooms,
mounts, settles to rhythmic pulsation
of a piston in perfect time. We wipe our
greasy hands on a soiled rag, drop tools
into the toolbox, push the Wheelhorse into the
garage, satisfied to have resurrected

a twelve-year-old tractor. It's early morning
when we close the garage door. Dew glistens
on branches of an apple tree. We part,
mutilated by fatigue, and I stare as his Camaro
disappears, my heart pulsating for more
than precision of machinery.

HOUSE

The man I married died today,
and all I imagined having for years is gone.

He was so right not to take for granted
our fleeting time of happiness as actual

as fidelity and the carpet under our feet.
We felt good about avoiding arguments

and mostly nodding in agreement,
spending Sunday nights enveloped

in mutual silence or reading to each other
from favorite books. Ours was a predictable

peace in a predictable house.

BURIED DESIRE AT BAYSIDE, MAINE

Weary of watching sails and shores,
I pull myself up from a wicker chair
in the living room of the house my friends
and I have rented for the week. Thinking
I'll take a nap or at least rest behind a book,

I sway up the stairs to my room.
Sun through the single window gouges
the room with amber light. I unlatch
the wooden frame, swing the window
outward. Through luminous glow I see
you sprawled on a canvas chair on the
patio next door, swim trunks the burnt
red of sangria. Your body shines with
sweat, miniscule mirrors or nanoscopic
bits of aluminum foil.

I want to wade into your shadow,
touch you. Instead, I slump to the foot
of my bed, unfulfillment stinging inside me.

All afternoon I watch you
apply oil, change positions, provide
a focal point for comparing my old age
to youth.

At a quarter to six, I shut the window,
descend stairs, join my friends on the front
porch. We watch fisherman on lobster boats

pull traps from the deep, sunset slowly melt
into dusk. People saunter along the tideline,
some hand in hand, others by themselves.
I reflect back to afternoon hours, secret
as memory, recount ascension of desire;
the uncontrollable sins of my eyes.

THE SNOWY OWL INN, NEW HAMPSHIRE

I check in, unpack, from the window of my room,
spot a path I want to follow. It leads up a rise
to woods, winds around the entire property,
punctuated at intervals by rest stations.
Younger men outstride my middle-age amble,
seem unaffected by July heat and humidity.
Short-winded, I complete the mile-long
loop that ends where it started.

I droop into an Adirondack chair
beside the indoor pool. Two men, I estimate to be
in their late twenties, linger in waist-high water,
close enough to each other to suggest more
than casual friendship. I slump behind a book
I'm not really reading, a white towel wrapped
around my flaccid midsection, embarrassed
by an under-exercised body. Determined to swim
alone, I wait for the men to leave.

They depart, and I drag myself from the chair,
swim ten laps from one side to the other.
I climb the ladder out of the pool. Water shingles
from me.

I grab the towel and book, stroll into the carpeted
lobby toward elevators, feel conspicuous wearing
only a swimsuit and flip flops, but it's a resort,
people in swimsuits a common sight. I unlock

the door to my room, peel off trunks. At the window,
hip-high sill hides my nakedness from tourists
unloading identical luggage. I would prefer
not to leave this room again until check-out time
in two days, but I've traveled here with friends
who would wonder about my isolation.
Intimidated by fathers and their youthful sons,
I retrieve pen and paper from my tote bag,
sag at the desk, attempt to write away
my lack of self-assurance, hope my unwavering pen
eliminates pangs of despondency and despair.

AVAILABLE LOVE FOR A WOMAN IN AUTUMN

He gives her the gift of tenderness,
finds her dark place, kisses her damp scent.

He whispers affectionate sentiments,
mouth glossy with possession.

Outside the window, snow accumulates
on clusters of bright-orange, bittersweet pods.

The yellow moon, no longer young, exudes
desolate light over corn shocks and a scarecrow

askew in an adjacent field. His body silkens
against hers, his reverent motion slightly

suspended, his inner touch an endless sacrament.
He opens her at the core. Gentle

undulations charge her spine. Arms wrapped
around his silhouette, she climbs to culmination.

Stillness follows, then a murmured appreciation
for his reachable nearness and his effort

to remove cold from her October sheets.

PIMP LUST

Jack Luckland, Romeo pimp, swagger's
out of Sweeney's jewelry store, bent over,
slightly crossing his legs in each step,
swinging his left arm. In his right hand
he carries a gift-wrapped box containing
a diamond gold Irish Celtic heart necklace
engraved with the name Louise.

It's snowing in Columbus, Ohio as if
a giant shredder has been turned upside
down on the city, and billions of white
snippets of paper cloud the air. Though
Jack wears a long, faux fur coat whiter
than the snow, beneath it he sports a
bottle-green velvet suit, sleeves, trousers
cuffed in a leopard pattern. His fedora
matches the snow, its brim ruffled by wind
as he struts arrogantly to his black Cadillac
Eldorado.

Louise had just turned fourteen when he lured her
from the school yard with promises of expensive
gifts, designer clothes, and a glamorous life.
She's been his bottom girl for ten years, and
the unthinkable has been progressively happening
to him. Would he call it love? No. That would mar
his stance as the most successful flesh peddler
in Columbus. He would lose control of his wifeys.
They would think him weak and fallible.

His soft spot for Louise makes him vulnerable
to his kind, and he can't afford such defacement.
Maybe he should throw the gold heart in the trash,
stop escalation of feelings for her before
he compromises identity.
This has never happened with any of his other
tattooed girls. Louise gives him inner peace,
makes him feel almost sacred. What can come of it?
It's only a gift, and there have been many
over the years to keep her under control.

Turmoil frustrates him as he climbs stairs
to her apartment, knocks on the door.
When she opens it, he hands her his heart.

PART THREE

All the world's a stage,
and all the men and women merely players.

William Shakespeare

SCENES FROM THE PUBLIC LIBRARY

A homeless man in a faded, plaid shirt yawns
behind a copy of *Newsweek*. Students
with heads bowed over books copy notes
onto legal pads, search for ready-made answers.

Several middle-aged women slouch
in overstuffed chairs, reading current novels.
Above them, skylights slant in November's
cold light. Odors of old paper, polished wood,

worn carpet, and binding glue scent the air.
The timid hide behind a book, experience life
at a safe distance, dispose of personal pain
a page at a time. At an oak table, a scholar

scrutinizes what the learned have written.
The discontented search for subversive literature,
ideas that will tilt the norm, while others wait
in the wings to censor them and draw the line

between what is and is not acceptable.
A young staff member with dreadlocks and
too much cleavage moseys away from her desk
to help a seemingly lost man retrieve journals

of Denton Welsh from the stacks. They amble
up and down rows of writing from the luminous
dead until she hands him what he is looking for.
All day, patrons wander in and out of the library,

bury themselves in second-hand knowledge
and the possibility of an unexpected hookup
amidst polite silence and the schliff sound
of turning pages.

MELTING

He ambles through the house, feels wasted
as spilled wine. The route he follows
from room to room at 3 a.m.
leads to temporary freedom from caring
for his ninety-two-year-old aunt who sleeps
in a bedroom cocooned in Alzheimer's.

He stops in the living room, gazes out
the window at snow-covered streets, thinks
if he stares long enough, he will see snow melt
along with responsibilities.

Next to the window, the fireplace is fireless,
its monotony of bricks rising from the floor
to the mantle on which a shelf clock ticks away
futile hours. A vapor light from across the street
beams a path over green carpet, silhouettes
coffee table, couch, chairs, despair. His life is
rigid with routine.

Prowling the house at this hour promises
a facsimile of freedom from the burden of being
custodian for the woman in the other room,
a moment to himself when he can breathe lighter.

In the morning, he will crumble bread
on the sidewalk for cold, December birds,
resume taking care of a life debilitated
by dreadful disease. For now, he pulls drapes shut
on quicksand he has waded into with no relief.

IDA LUPINO IN LAMPLIGHT

(actress, writer, director 1918-1995)

She raises the Lucky Strike to her lips,
cigarette holder held between two fingers,
remembers 1934 when her 16-year-old
throat swelled with soreness.

She figured it was just a common symptom
of the flu. Bones ached. Fever soared.
Neck stiffness, vomiting, and intestinal pain
precipitated a diagnosis of polio. It was
a mild case, and she survived.   Authorities
agreed it was the result of contaminated
swimming pool water in Hollywood.

She flips glowing embers into an ashtray,
lights another cigarette, thinks about
her reluctance to play ingenue rolls, prefers
to play a prostitute or a hard-hitting mama
with a gun in hand.

August 1993, colon cancer creeps into her life
like an insidious snake. She's stretched out
on the examining table when the stroke
brings her life to an end.

She inhales from the cigarette, worries
that smoke will intrude on the picture
she is framing with her camera.

She is a prolific and respected director now,
bad things behind her until the stroke
interrupted colon-cancer treatment
in Los Angeles on August 3rd, 1995.

She stubs the cigarette out, lights one more,
her death, another film noir, she couldn't direct
with her usual renegade expertise.

ADRIFT

Friends laugh at me when I tell them
there is such a thing as a pushy half-moon.
It bloats lust, prompts half-baked poetry,
bends a person backwards over the possibility
of love. I'd rather stay frozen with terrible desire
than be trapped in its unforgiving light.

Many times I've ogled it through poverty
of skid-row eyes, a vagrant of my own
drunk-addled loneliness. Even as
I've slouched against a brick wall in an alley,
veins full of electric booze, I've mistrusted
it's beauty, it's cape of illumination
that covered me like yellow broth. Why
did I ever think life might satisfy me?
I could have been a music teacher or
a practitioner for the sick, but I shuffled through
young cutouts of myself, way back when,
eliminated the good, fell to my knees for drugs
and dereliction.

These days, exhausted from hearing the naked
scream of failure in my head, I crawl
from handout to handout, sprawl on concrete
of a Speedway station. It's too late in my life
for intimacy, so the moon's interference
doesn't count anymore, doesn't rev up pink heat

of my brain. In moments of delirium, I dream
of a summer shore where waves, the color of iron,
strike land, and I am a corpse lost
in choppy undercurrent.

DRUNKEN HOURS STOLE FROM ETERNITY

You rip open a bag of pork rinds,
uncap a bottle of Yuengling.
Perched on a loveseat in front of your computer,
you sip until the screen becomes blurry,
the image inconsequential. What is important
is the deliberate obliteration of the clock,
defiance against necessity to sleep.
Genesis of such rebellion stems from years
when school attendance forced you to be in bed
by 10:00 p.m. Thereafter, thirty years of teaching
shortened evenings to a reasonable bedtime.
Staying up late is a gift of retirement.

You nestle into a boozy haze, a cozy cocoon,
a solitary displacement of self. You stand up,
grab the arm of a nearby chair, wobble
into the kitchen for your fifth beer. Maybe
you're cutting life short with such behavior,
but intoxication and dissent from the norm
is too delicious to resist.

You trudge carefully back to the loveseat
which is big enough for two people, even so,
you prefer to be alone in this insular celebration,
inebriated on a self-made island.

You awaken six hours later without any memory
of having blanked out. Unconsciousness occurred
faster than one heartbeat. You stare at the computer
where a screensaver of the Mojave Desert prevented
anyone from viewing desktop contents
while you swooned into an oblivious stupor, an untold
number of empties overflowing the wastebasket.

AMATEUR BLUES

I sip a Coors in Nashville, waiting
in the airport for flight 443.
I traveled down here to play guitar.
Lovers and insomnia used up many nights,
gave music of a loner back to me. Later,
I will scribble a lyric about
my undiscovered talent and how
all I ever wanted falls down to nothing
like the rain tonight. A dogwood branch,
outside the terminal's window, catches
shiny drops, rough-cut diamonds bloated
with waiting-room fluorescence.
Does my face show I'd just as least
have another beer as go home a failure?
So, I'll have another beer. Time I slowed down.
Time I realized there's something troubling
about a headache only beer can soothe.
Yesterday is bleached out, an albino memory,
yesterday of weeks ago when I came to Nashville
to blurt out a song and be discovered.

I snap myself into an airplane seat, ask myself,
"Where are you?" Answer, "Hell, I don't know.
I think I'm heading back North, maybe to write
a song about a man lying beside the road,
a man I saw two days ago dying or just resting
like me." I stretch back, fold my hands in my lap,
listen to the power of flight surround the plane

and take me home to a one-gas-station town,
the entrance ramp of which leads to a life
of heads or tails, to a wife who will say,
"I could have told you you're mediocre before you left."

CHOKING

Madeline hides the beginning of belly fat
beneath a mint-green, silk printed, twist dress,
saunters into Glazer's Restoration Restaurant,
orders a glass of Cold Duck, handmade pasta,
and a dinner salad. While the waiter jots notes,
she stretches her neck to make sag
of middle-aged skin disappear, unfolds a napkin,
white as a June cloud, spreads it over her lap.

Minutes later, the waiter returns with wine
and a salad. She lifts a fork, and the glint
 of its beauty goes to her mouth. Swallowing
the third forkful, lettuce lodges in her throat.
She begins coughing, and the waiter surges
across the room to her table. Her eyes are
frozen open. He phones 911. Four medics
rush in, surround her like parasites
on a helpless host. Other diners, distracted
from meals, hesitantly resume eating.
Medics perform the Heimlich maneuver,
pamper her back to recovery. So pallid
is her skin, makeup appears over applied,
lipstick smeared like a red tire burn.
Medics repack their equipment, pause
for a last look, depart. She smooths her
disheveled dress, straightens herself out
the best she can under public scrutiny.
The waiter announces there will be no charge
for the dinner, compliments of management

along with regrets about the unfortunate incident.
She thanks him, pulls back her chair. Outside,
she waits for Uber, fingers her Kate Spade
handbag, grips it like life.

A SHADOWY TALE OF SUMMER

Two preteen boys drowned fishing off the damn
one summer day. I always remember
that accident when driving on Greenlawn
Avenue along the Scioto River.

Plenty of people fish there. These boys
were by themselves, perhaps hoping
for a catch that would be much talked about.

I picture them wearing baseball caps,
taking an occasional look up, squinting
into intense sun. They lay bait can and
stringer on shore, took small steps
into shallow water that slipped over the dam
like liquid silk, frothed and foamed
as if full of detergent when it hit the river.

One boy's line snagged on a drifted log.
It must have frightened him to wade into
fringe of surf below the dam, but he did.
Undercurrent sucked him beneath the surface.
He grabbed at water. The other boy attempted
rescue, followed the first into riptide.

A passerby saw the struggle.
By the time he notified authorities, both
boys had disappeared. Fishing lines leaped,
tossed in the current, frantic, convulsive jerks,
alive above the dead
they later dragged the bottom for.

FANTASY ON THE DEATH OF SYLVIA PLATH

One draft is all death gets from her,
no revision, just perfect first lines.

In the kitchen, china rattles with words.
Jelly jars darken with syllables.

Her breath is imprisoned in the tea cup,
throat dry as old crockery.

Her mind bulges with metaphors.
Figures of speech lie open in her eyes.

No shrieks. No wails.
Her head is quiet as stone, surrounded

by four black walls. She has written
the brain's scenery, suffered like burns,

let hooves of language fly over her
as if they were on velvet horses.

She says a prayer, smooth
as a mouth would be in love.

Gas rolls from the oven, touches her.
The undertaker props her jaw open,

picks out jagged jot notes from her
swollen tongue, exhales his own breath

of bourbon and mercy.

INFAMOUS LANTERN

Light flares across ceiling beams of the barn
when Catherine O'Leary ratchets up the wick
of the Lantern placed on an empty crate.
She squats on a stool in Daisy's stall,
firmly holds Daisy's teat between thumb and
forefinger, draws down the full length of the teat,
at the same time presses to make milk flow
into the metal bucket.

It was a stifling summer, so the breeze that rattles
through Chicago on this evening of October 9th,
1871 brings much relief. The barn, packed with fuel
and animal feed, quakes a bit more with an increase
in wind, making Daisy more nervous than usual.
A fortuitous twitch and then a kick of her hind leg
topples the lantern. Straw flares with flame,
an instantaneous inferno.

The blaze at 137 DeKoven Street spreads to a city
six miles long and three miles wide. Fire engines
arrive twenty minutes later. The conflagration
devastates an area four miles long and three-quarters
of a mile deep.

Catherine races to her house, meets her husband,
Patrick, in the doorway. It appears their home
will be spared.

The fire lasts three days, and on the third day,
a miracle of rain helps quench flames.

As weeks pass, most fingers in town point
to Catherine as the cause of three hundred people
dead, thousands homeless, and the destruction
of 3.3 square miles of the city.
When she approaches the spot where the barn was,
she weeps for incalculable loss, spots the dome of
the lantern protruding from a pile of ash.

NOTHING LEFT BUT THE NINE O' CLOCK DIVE

John balances on the tip of the diving board
beneath sky, a hand with a fingerprint of moon
on its thumb. He stares down at blue water
now black as darkness, straightens arms out
parallel to his destination. Smooth as milk
spilling from a glass, he falls through furious air,
disappears below an ebony surface that
splashes open around his body like a watery
entrance to warm silence. He dog paddles
to pool's edge, shakes scrollwork of the moon
from wet hair, holds onto the concrete ledge,
thinks about his dead friend, Jim, with whom
he swam in this pool last summer.

Jim, a paratrooper, died during practice maneuvers
when his plane crashed over a cornfield
in Wilmington, Ohio. They had trespassed over
the chain link fence that John had climbed tonight
to swim in a private pool belonging to Millbrook
Apartments.

John loosens himself from memory, climbs
out of the water, grabs his towel, clambers back
over the fence away from remembrance
and lingering grief of a lost passion.

MISERY OF THE MONARCH

The Coronation

Anne Stuart's limbs burn with painful inflammation.
Gout disables her ability to walk, so her Lady-in-waiting
summons the specially designed open sedan chair
to carry the future queen to Westminster Abbey.
At thirty-seven, she is just too unwell and overweight
to walk the processional route of four hundred feet
from Westminster Hall to the Abbey. Humbled
by her infirmity, but stalwart, she receives the crown
and the affirmation of royalty. After the ceremony,
at the garden party, she is awkward and shy
at impromptu conversation, moves her lips
without utterance, stares at guests with watery eyes.

The Death

In 1713, gout stops Anne from walking altogether.
Thereafter, she uses a wheelchair. After several
severe strokes, her doctors treat her with bleeding,
blistering, hot irons, and garlic on the feet, a procedure
that causes her insufferable pain. At 7:45 a.m.
on Sunday, August 1st, 1714, Anne dies at Kensington
Palace. She is forty-nine, the last of the Stuarts.
Her body lies at the palace for three weeks, so swollen
with dropsy that she has to be interred in a vast,
square-shaped coffin 14 carpenters have to carry.
John Arbuthnot, one of her doctors, writes
to Jonathan Swift "I believe sleep was never more
welcome to a weary traveller than death was to her."

THE SERPENTINE

John Levesley, a pensioner of the Chelsea Hospital,
turns up the collar of his greatcoat against howling
gusts of December wind, pulls his bowler hat down
tighter. On his way to Kensington, he cuts through
Hyde Park, from the corner of his eye spots
something afloat in the Serpentine Lake. A closer
look reveals a young woman's body. He notifies
authorities, and they transport the corpse to the
Fox and Bull inn on Knightsbridge where a hastily
convened inquest pronounces the verdict of suicide.

Harriet Westbrook Shelley left behind a sad note
addressed to her father, sister, and husband
in which she expresses her intention to commit
suicide because her husband, Percy, has left her.
She does not, of course, mention her own
unfaithfulness as the cause of his departure.
Pregnant, allegedly with Percy's child, she forgives
him, wishes him a happy life. Within the note,
the depth of her despair reveals itself through
disjointed lines, poor spelling, and broken grammar.

Rumors circulate that she has taken a lover,
a Major Ryan, captain in the Indian army.
With increasing evidence of her pregnancy,
she flees her parent's house, takes lodgings
in Hans Place, Knightsbridge, tells the landlady
her husband is abroad. Despondent and disgraced,
she eventually succumbs to prostitution,

lives with a groom named Smith, becomes
a person suffering ignominy, dishonor, social stigma,
with no dignified choice left but to endure
the finality of death.

ELEGANCE

Fred Astaire can't keep his feet still
even on a crowded street. He steps out

on mid-air, taps flashing a practiced move,
executes routines until he's blind with fatigue.

Solos polished to perfection, he sways,
twirls, whirls, frolics on ceilings, wrestles hat racks,

sidesteps firecrackers, glides into a carriage beside
Cyd Charisse. June 22, 1987, sun glitters

on Los Angeles palm fronds as
the ultimate choreographer appears, and,

in the arms of his wife, Robyn, death,
a dance-hall harlot, two-steps Fred off stage.

CHOPIN'S HEART

Chopin lies in a canopy bed in Paris, dying.
He is wasted to ninety-nine pounds, pale
as a trumpeter swan, has lain unconscious
for the previous twenty-four hours.
An army of doctors have tended
to his physical ailments which include
a continual cough, fever, painful ankles
and wrists, hemoptsis, hematemesis, and
ankle edema.

Wednesday, mid-morning of December 17th,
1849, he rallies enough to allow Clesinger
to make a death mask and a cast of his left arm
which he favored in many of his compositions.
His sister, Ludwika, slumps beside the bed,
holds his hand. He prays, calls out to God,
refuses confession, says he does not believe in it.
He asks for a paper and pen, scribbles
"As this earth will suffocate me, I implore you
to have my body opened so that I will not be
buried alive." Fearful of awakening
in his own coffin, he entreats Ludwika
to have his heart removed after his death
and sent to Warsaw, his homeland.

A little past midnight, a physician leans
over his thirty-nine-year-old patient, asks
if Chopin is in great pain? "Not anymore,"
he answers.

EMPTY TRAPEZE

Thirty years old, he is no stranger
to the desire to fly. He clips on
a safety belt, climbs a rope ladder
toward a canvas heaven, mesh
at the top of the tent hot as a beach
in July.

He reaches the small platform
that sways a little under his feet,
lifts the bar off the hook, swings
forward for a wrist to wrist grip
with the catcher. For this matinee,
they work without a safety net, soar
back and forth like radiant birds
until a cramp in the catcher's wrist
causes him to let go. He grasps
the flyer by one arm, holds tight
until strength runs out, and their hands
slip apart from the promised catch.
The audience gasps when the flyer
crashes to the ground.

An ambulance speeds to the scene.
Paramedics lift the body with a
broken neck onto a stretcher,
place the flyer's head on a pillow
soft as chance.

GUN STREET

Owen tucks the Glock Model 199mm pistol
behind his Levi waistband in the appendix
region, a firearm he purchased for $350
from his best friend, Logan, whose arsenal
of stolen guns and stash house of drugs
affords delinquents and malefactors cut-rate
deals in exchange for their dependence on him.
Logan's impudent swagger and readiness
to transact illegal business has made him
a kingpin in the urban neighborhood of Kingston.
At the moment, he specializes in Tianeptine,
known as gas station heroin, as well
as regular heroin, and the latter is what Owen
plans to purchase from his drug-peddling friend.

Owen steps from his front porch, takes long strides
toward the dilapidated house Logan rents. He knocks
on the front door. Logan doesn't pull back
the bed sheet that covers the door's window
to reveal a suspicious but impish grin.
Owen knocks again without a response.
On the off chance, he turns the knob, and
the door opens. Owen hesitates inside,
creeps through the empty living room toward
the bedroom. He turns the knob on the shut door.
It opens to reveal Owen's wife who quickly
pulls a blanket up to cover her naked body.
Shock on Logan's face turns cranberry red.
"It's not what it looks like," Logan bellows,

ripping out of bed, wearing nothing but underwear.
The wife, as if hit by a thunderbolt, is stunned
into silence, her face white as the inside
of a clamshell. Owen whips the gun
from his waistband. Logan twists the gun
from Owen's hand. Owen doesn't speak,
turns toward the door, tromps outside.
Logan follows him to the entrance, continues
to shout, "I can explain. I can explain."
Owen doesn't stop or look back.
Numbness fills his mind as if an invisible
hand we're squeezing his brain into non-existence.
As though he had swallowed a tray of ice,
the chill of betrayal freezes his gut.
Without any reluctance he takes out a mental pencil,
x's out the two most important people in his life.

THE PRIVILEGED ON PAWLEYS ISLAND

Sailboats pitch toward Pawleys Island,
drop anchors in July. Sun bites down
on shoulders of the rich, tans them
beneath expensive oils. Abalone, costly
flower arrangements, the slow assent
of a match to a candle, and the table is
set for human faces to astound each other
with unmatched conversation and etiquette.

Rising at 6:00 a.m., the advantaged swing
into Gucci's and Calvin Klein's, walk
Afghan hounds, Akitas, and Welsh Corgis
along shoreline. Refined barks command
owners from retractable leashes.

On the patio of a luxurious condo,
two women lunch at a Comino aluminum
dining set, sip sweetness from lemonade
and gossip.

Meanwhile, at the north causeway,
their husbands, avid anglers, catch speckled
trout and flounder with a Daiwa Dendoh
Marine Power Fishing Reel.

Above the Atlantic tideline, several teenage boys,
clad in $430 Backstroke Edition swimsuits,
hunt for banded tulip shells. Later,
they will lounge upon a MasterCraft, handcrafted

yacht followed by a flock of gulls looking for life
below water's surface.

This colony of the affluent
strolls the beach for hours, aloof
from the dispossessed, live luminous lives,
find the earth a pleasure.

EMILY DICKINSON DELINEATION

She resists lure of the spring afternoon
the way her hand resists thorns
when she snips roses from the rosarium,
pulls down the blind to shut out sexless sun.
Below the bay box sash window
of the two-and-a half-story, brick house,
Austin's adolescent children, Ned, Martha,
and Gib have settled on the grass, chatter
to each other. Her brother has warned them
not to bother their aunt, yet Emily thinks
the children wait for her to lower love
to them as if it were on a string.
Sometimes, their aunt reads to them
from *Grimm's Fairy Tales* or the family Bible,
but she prefers silence and solitude.

Though having a penchant for browns, wools,
and calico prints, now in her thirties,
she wears only a white dress. Townspeople joke
about her attire, call her the myth.

This evening, she bends over her square,
eighteen-inch table, retrieves ink bottle, paper,
and pen from a deep drawer, and in her unique style
of extensive dots, dashes, and unconventional
capitalization, scribbles "Because I could not stop
for Death, He kindly stopped for me…"

She turns up the wick on the oil lamp.
Shadows hang on walls like black draperies.
She continues to write, a scribe of the soul,
self-imprisoned by imaginary bars.

THE ORGANIST

In a white shirt and light-blue trousers, you lean
over the keyboard, fingers selecting notes
that hang in the air, excite your connection
between music and sex. You want to remove
your clothes as you said you had once done
in a belfry-like room hidden from the congregation,
your penis growing with each stroke and vibration.

Today, you are clothed and pure
to the eye, play like an expert typist,
find keys as easily as you would a lover in the dark.
You have memorized arrangements for weddings
and high Mass, said that while you play
you are certain eyes of the priest massage your back,
lay small touches on your shoulders, invite you
to show him how to rid himself of forbidden ardor.
This is the way you go about your work, fondle
the urge to tell him all you know about impure
flesh and impulse.

On the way home, a secret hunger spreads
from belly to bones. You cruise past McDonald's
drive-thru window, order a hamburger, park,
tilt back your seat, and stare through the windshield
at empty branches and fallen leaves.

ENSLAVED PRAYER

An appalling gloom descends on Gambian huts
as slave traders battle villagers into leg irons,
linking the innocent together in a chain of futility.
A husky slaver wrestles a seven-year-old girl
away from her mother who clings to her daughter
like barnacles on a rock. The child loses her grip
on her mother's waist, is shoved onto the New
England Brigantine Phillis, given a shelf to lie on
with barely enough room to fit her body.
Women scream giving birth, newborns tossed
to sharks, placenta left for rats. Of the ninety-six
Africans, enslaved and forced aboard, seventy-five
survive the 245-day voyage to Boston.

The ship docks in Boston Harbor,
and the little gap-tooth girl, wrapped in pieces
of dirty carpet, is shoved onto the auction block.
The Wheatleys, John and Susanna, loiter
at the base of the platform, assessing
the newly-arrived slaves. Susanna says she wants
the little girl, will pay as much as a thousand dollars
for her. The Wheatleys call her Phillis after the ship
she came in on.

They help the girl into their carriage, head home,
not knowing yet they had purchased a child prodigy
who in a few years would become one of the first

black and enslaved persons in the United States
to publish a book of poems and pen the lines,
"Such, such my case. And can I then but pray
Others may never feel tyrannic sway?"

PART FOUR

Where there is no imagination,
there is no horror.

Arthur Conan Doyle

There is something at work in my soul
which I do not understand.

Mary Shelley

THE INFLUENCE OF HORROR FILMS ON A SUBURBAN HUSBAND

His wife has taken the kids for a weekend
at her mother's. The weatherman forecasts
severe storms. It's 10:30 a.m. and
he is slumped on a stool in the kitchen eating
a bowl of All Bran. The first, distant rumbling
is a bowling ball traveling the length
of a hardwood alley. Having the house
to himself, this is the time to test the truth
of what he believes from watching double
features at drive-in movies as an adolescent.
He remembers a coil of rope on the workbench
in the garage. Back in the kitchen, he rips
the polka-dotted, cafe curtain from the window
as the first javelin of lightning tears the sky,
ties himself to the kitchen table he has cleared
with a single sweep of an arm. He eats lightning
that continues to illuminate the room. Each pore
galvanized, his skull grows, overhangs eyebrows.
He morphs into a hirsute creature, opens his mouth
to see if there will be any sound. A growl rolls
from his tongue. As if he'd drunk a bottle of Geritol,
new strength pops the rope. He lumbers toward
the living room, knows now the movies weren't lying.
It seems the unstoppable storm might last for years.
It's the kind of storm that bites trees out of the ground,
that sheets the world with rain a person can only
stumble through. He staggers into the living room.
His furry hand clutches the front-door knob when

the phone rings. He paws the receiver from its cradle.
His wife forgot the grocery list, wants to know
if he can locate it and read it to her. She plans
to do weekly shopping before she returns, asks
if he is alright. Infringing on him at the height
of his manliness, he slams the phone down,
mouth twisted as if he'd just sipped ammonia.
He reaches for the doorknob again, twists it,
lurches into the gray rain, swallowing lightning,
living for the next full moon,
flapping a strip of polka-dotted curtain
stuck to the bottom of his shoe.

BET

I open my notebook, quill pen in hand,
begin to write the nightmarish story
I dreamed last night, June 16th, 1816,
about a scientist who created life,
horrified by what he had created.

I could not sleep, vivid images kept rolling
through my mind, imagination tossed
and turned me until I had an idea.
I will call it *Frankenstein* or *The Modern
Prometheus*.

I turn up an oil lamp, light a candle.
My eighteen-year-old hand continues to scribble
words in answer to Lord Byron's challenge
of two nights ago: who among you can write
the best horror story? Percy, Lord Byron, Dr. John
Polidori, Claire Clairmont, and I lounge
in front of the stone fireplace. The crackle
of flaming logs does not mask thunderclaps
of an impending storm outside the villa Diodati
on the shore of Lake Geneva, Switzerland.
The room is rife with shadows, ghost stories,
 and the spirit to compete.

I finish chapter one, rub my eyes, turn down
the lamp, blow out the candle, apprehensive
but hopeful I'll have a decent chance
to win the competition.

THE FAILED TENDERNESS OF VICTOR FRANKENSTEIN

The beauty of discovery can kill
he speculates on the day he discovers
the secret of life at the University
of Ingolstadt, Germany. He wants
to create life from death, knows this
will not be popular because of the
implication that he is playing God.
So, he sets up his laboratory in a
chamber at the top of his house, an
eerie space lit by flickering candles
that cast shadows on the walls. Test
tubes, viles, electrical machinery clutter
tables, while shelves hold jars of
unusual specimens. Victor begins
his experiment by collecting human
body parts from charnel-houses, dissecting
rooms, and the slaughterhouse.

Secrecy an utmost priority, he assembles
a second lab in a miserable hut he rents
on the remotest island in the Orkneys
off the Scottish Coast. The hut has two rooms,
unplastered walls, and a broken door, but
it is here, after two laborious years of work,
that the nineteen-year-old finally brings
his creature to life through a combination
of chemistry, anatomy, and electricity.

The monster stirs, and Victor sinks
against the wall, repulsed, disgusted, horrified
by his own creation, wants to distance himself
from this eight-foot creature. The monster
calls Victor father, says Victor is responsible
for him, that people will be unkind, that
he will be miserable, and that Victor, himself,
will run away because his own creation is so ugly.

Months later, having found no goodness
in humanity, the monster kills Victor,
weeps over his dead creator's body.
Abandoned, without a real relationship,
the monster contemplates suicide, speaks and
acts like a grieving son toward a lost parent.

VICTOR FRANKENSTEIN ON THE EDGE OF AFFECTION

There is cause to believe his intention is good
at the outset but recedes each day from an
experiment for the welfare of mankind
to a passion for usurping the best secrets of God.

He carries pieces of death from the charnel house
into his laboratory, makes an artificial man
that walks and talks however awkwardly,
a creature with the heart of a human.

The creature answers questions it has been taught
polite society will ask. Crowds are struck
by the creature's beauty. Rumors spread of
royal blood. Romance fills the eyes of aspirant
young ladies. All the while, suspicion never arises
that the creature's delicate hands have ever been stained
by death.

The creature and its maker become companions,
but, blind with triumph, the doctor doesn't notice
the creature's mouth becoming toothless, it's hair
dropping into the sun's rays, it's face festering
with first signs of decay.

Humiliation blows about the doctor's brain like dry leaves,
but never does he consider his creation lies sleepless
in another room, holding back the sound of anguish,
wondering why the doctor's strong hands have not
made him well.

Deterioration continues. The doctor keeps the creature
secluded. Each day, the creature waits for the doctor
to bring him back to what he had been, to a time
when the softness of patience with each other had yielded
a solution to empty solitude.

The creature stops eating, loses all hunger
for food but starts feeding on itself because
of a deep urge to destroy its empty stomach,
its ugly head, its borrowed heart. Quite suddenly
it appears at the doctor's door, beseeching
as it never had, begging as it never will again,
softly, entreats, "Victor, help me."
The doctor hears his name spoken, closes a book
he is reading, looks at the shrunken face, thinks,
"He was so beautiful once," but says, "I can't."
The creature wraps his hands around the doctor's
throat, squeezes him into unconsciousness
with a surprising reserve of strength, then
gently lifts the limp body in his arms, calling it father.

Victor awakens, his head full of yellow light,
his shirt sweat-soaked. He stumbles into motion,
drunk with revenge, tromps across polar ice fields
of the Arctic Circle where whiteness has no edges.
Stiff with cold, he cannot feel his own hands,
has no warm breath to blow into them. His lips are
cracked with cold, bleed, ask for nothing not even
a last chance against the hopeless thing he has created.
In the distance, a grotesque face watches landscape
teach survival. The creature throws back his head,
screams into white chaos, "Victor, yours is the greater sin."

MORGAN INSANE ASYLUM, 1750

Colin Collier prays for a window and fresh air,
but he has been shoved into a rubber room
because of obsessive talk about escape.
His older brother, Kern, committed Colin
to Morgan when Colin turned eighteen.
Kern couldn't manage Colin's melancholia,
the younger brother's interminable depression
and sadness, his constant strolling by the sea,
deep in thought.

Colin's twenty-two-year-old shoulders slump
as he slouches on a wooden bench in the dark.
He has heard screams of patients who have faced
electroshock, ice baths, forced drugging,
and even lobotomies. When he mentions the sea,
attendants rope him into restraints. He breaks
free only in his imagination, sees his feet turn
to sprigs of seaweed, ocean wet while above,
a spine of sky holds up the sun, a pumpkin face
bruised with clouds, that broods its distant light
on him.

This day, he lied to an attendant about
what he really wanted: asked of intentions, he said
suicide when he really meant seaside.
Deprived of food for three days, his body bends
limp as a willow branch. His brain wallows
in distortions, makes a delusional boat
into which he flops out of despair, sees freedom
and the froth of ocean at the edge of his eyes.

PART FIVE

My name is Rita. What does it mean?

RITA'S WRONG LOVE

Kind days dwindle as she tries to understand
why her fingers are spread open on the bed
in a grip of quiet despair, and why
she has arisen in the middle of the night
to fix a bowl of cereal brightened by streetlight?
Why in the morning does she hunch over
her office desk, typing other people's letters,
the giant clock telling her the future has already
passed?

At 5:00 p.m., she retrieves her purse
from the lower desk drawer, feels
her usual belly-crawling desire to be
cared for. Outside her apartment,
she snaps the stem of a Queen Elizabeth
rose, finds a suitable vase.

That night, she pushes a hand up the wall,
arm straight, pointing at the ceiling, blood,
bone, and flesh high as a flag, waits for sleep
to drain down to her chest like a caress.
She thinks how easy it would be to die,
turn the soul away, draw knees up, dismiss life.
But now, everywhere she looks, her need
for love multiplies on the glitter of jewelry,
the door knobs, the yellow bedspread covering
numbness.

She rises from a surreal dream, slumps
at her desk, writes a poem inspired by the dream
about the body's need to step out of a clown suit.
The poem is an amateur act, full of personal truth
but riddled with clichés embarrassing as an unwanted
gift.

The next morning, an office boy at work
gives her a sheath of poems to evaluate.
She has feelings for this man

who has handed over his work for her
approval. She tells him that his poems
contain enough candor to toss her all night
from one side of her bed to another.
She knows she is foolish for letting herself
begin to fall for a man ten years her junior.

A few days later, he hands her more poems,
these about his wife and twin sons vacationing
in a Minnesota cabin.

At home, Rita rips the pages to pieces. In bed,
she wraps darkness around her thighs, breasts,
shoulders. Her head spins as if after a drink
too many. His words are gentle as a soft rain,
but they nullify the possibility of any romance.
During a restless night, she realizes
she must accept their meanings by morning.

RITA'S RECENT DATE

She lays middle age aside tonight,
moistens lips, pushes through the door
of Oak Leaves Lounge. December cold
spirals in behind her. She seats herself
at a table across from her boss at
Copeland Electric Company.
He comments on her blood-red lipstick
reminiscent of Marilyn Monroe's glossy pout,
comments that nothing is above revival.
They order filet mignon, roasted vegetables,
mashed potatoes, and Pinot Noir.
Deep into their first date, spurts of laughter
punctuate friendly chat. They eat, talk,
avoid awkward silence, but that's exactly
what descends on their effort to keep the date
buoyant. The seams of desperation begin
to show on the dress of her self-confidence.
Conversation turns awkward as if suddenly
both wonder why they are there.

He walks her to her Hyundai Elantra,
touches his hand to her cheek but doesn't kiss her.
She steers home past endless streetlights,
the East River, dreams of dissolving solitude.

In her driveway, she kills the engine, lolls
against the seat, pulls a souvenir cocktail napkin
from her purse. She will lay the napkin on her
dresser next to Ralph Lauren's Romance, a perfume
she will be wary to give anybody a chance
to breathe again.

RITA'S MOTHER RETREATS INTO ALZHEIMER'S

Rita grabs her purse, locks the front door,
twists the knob to check for security.
Neighbors stand nearby on the sidewalk,
eyes puffy from early awakening, splashed red
from the intermittent cycle of ambulance light.
Rita's mother, strapped to a stretcher, rises
on a hydraulic lift into the back of the ambulance.
Inside the vehicle, Rita slouches on an imitation
leather bench. A young attendant with tight facial
skin and prominent cheekbones sits stiff as a nail
across from her. The ambulance bumps into motion,
accelerates away from the curb, enters traffic,
strident siren insisting on a safe path. Paramedics
wheel Rita's mother past double doors
into the emergency room of Mount Carmel Hospital.
Starched atmosphere seems sacred as an Indian temple.
Rita fills out paperwork, thinks how her old mother's
life has been reduced to pencil marks.

A month later, February snow builds high mounds
of white across the city. Back home, Rita's mother
resumes a facsimile of housekeeping, squeezes a lemon
at the sink, age spots on her hands accentuated by winter
sunlight through the kitchen window. Afterwards,
she roams the house in spite of swollen ankles, wonders
why she has saved yellow juice, can't find the empty rind
anywhere in the living room. She wanders back
to the kitchen table where Rita waits,

forgetfulness sitting down to breakfast with them.
Rita wears responsibility of caregiver like a too-tight
garment, independence replaced by fear, acceptance
that she must assume the role of parent
while the ghost of her freedom dies in her helpless arms.

RITA'S WEAKNESS

She shuts down the office in which she works
as a secretary in the Copeland Insurance Company
in downtown Columbus, heads to Lazarus
department store to take pleasure in caressing
faux fur coats, an indulgence she allows herself
once a month on payday. The Friday crowd
has begun to populate the parking garage, but
she finds a space for her blue Hyundai Elantra
and parks. Head down against a March snow
squall, she trudges to the store's entrance,
takes an escalator to the fourth floor where
an array of fur coats glisten under fluorescent light.
She runs her hand down the sleeve of a black,
fur hooded teddy, soft as hope, wraps herself
in a brown, shearling jacket. She swoons,
light-headed from luxury, from the tingle
of satisfaction. Next, she slips into a white,
lapel neck coat, studies herself in a floor-length
mirror, wants to live in this coat. A sales clerk
surfaces from nowhere, asks if she can help.
Rita shakes off a stare, says "No. I'm just looking."
The sales clerk suggests trying on a different coat.
Rita's mouth is dry from anticipation. She can only
think, "Yes," tunnels one arm at a time into mid- length,
winter plush. Rita stands erect, feels as if she is filling in
for someone else's life. She turns, rehearsing a new self,
transformed, the Phoenix after the flame, self-doubt dispelled.
Rita is so concentrated on herself as a newborn lady
that she doesn't hear the salesperson purring beside her,

offering Rita the chance to keep the feeling of this strange
love on her shoulders forever. The salesperson admires
aloud the coat's workmanship, says of its beauty
how easy it is to want. Rita stops turning, raises her arms,
makes it easy for the clerk to remove the coat
from this shopper's possession. Emptiness floods
Rita's stomach, a testimony to the return to an ordinary self,
to the emergence from a moment of transformation
back to a person not special or different in any way.

THE FUTILITY OF RITA'S FALSE LIFE

She feeds her fingers ninety words per minute
at the computer keyboard. The manager is pleased,
and she takes pleasure in his praise. Ever since
his marriage and fatherhood, he's taken
the padlock off his heart, seems especially sensitive
to secretaries' salaries and the need for swivel chairs.
He looks at the correspondence she types,
holds each page at a distance to accommodate
his farsightedness.

Today, however, she fidgets, clutches arms
of her chair, feels movement in her stomach.
She straightens, resumes typing, waits to see
if what is sleeping in the pouch of her belly
will move again. It does, and she rises
from her chair, whirls of dizziness accompanying
her to the restroom. She locks the door,
presses both palms to her abdomen.
Can she dare to believe the movement within her
is another's life, magic within her possible
without a man's love, without the pressing inward
of an embrace she hasn't had for years?
She wants to sob, to sing, to hug the walls
as she bears the weightless kick of bliss within
her womb. When movement inside her subsides,
she returns to her desk, the day's work glossed over,
pushed aside. Stirring in her stomach starts again
as she shrugs into her coat.

For days, she feels hope kicking her,
eats more carefully, flattens hands against herself
to feel the obligation of tending to a newborn.
For days, she leaps into her work, throbs with passion
of being needed, polices files for over-looked claims
and fraudulent ones that have been submitted
to the Copeland Insurance Company.
Not once does she lose sight of being
on the threshold of receiving God's riches.

For over a week, fetal messages in her body
do not stop. Then, one night, in bed awake,
waves of anticipation rolling through her mind,
all activity within her ceases. Fear of loss washes
ashore from a great ocean of disappointment.
She rises from bed, taste of defeat salty
on her tongue, feels bitter about the snub of fate.
Morning light of a lightless day crawls onto sheets,
lies beside her body curled into a tight, prenatal position.

RITA'S DESIRES IN A HOUSE OF DENIALS

She sifts a handful of flour onto flattened dough
beneath pressure of the rolling pin, thinks of years
lived without creating a pie that pleases her mother
who insists Rita treat the crust with shyness,
touch it as little as possible. Apples from the Jonagold
tree in the backyard lay sliced and ready.

Middle-aged, unmarried, Rita wishes to meet
the mythological man whose instant attraction
will afford love without end, but she is compelled
as sole caregiver to forgo socialization and tend
night and day to her mother's Alzheimer's condition.
Her only romance occurs when she stirs hope
into the mix, embraces a bowl, a spoon, a saucepan,
aspires to become the perfect cook who can prepare
food to satisfy her parent.

Rita places the pie on the rack of a fifty-year-old
gas oven, sets the temperature at 350.
Her mother says Rita's pies are never right.
They're always a little too much or a little too less
of an ingredient that would make them acceptable.
Her mother's objections loom in Rita's mind,
criticism as real as a dirty spoon on a clean tablecloth.

She's been ready for twenty years to receive
a stranger's kiss, the one she only imagines
after years of anticipation and useless recipes.
She touches her lips with fingertips.

The pie is almost done. She wishes for a faultless result
and the possibility of a man's arms around her,
such things can happen, although her mother
will never acknowledge their possibility.

PART SIX

If you want your children to be intelligent,
read them fairy tales. If you want them
to be more intelligent, read them more fairy tales.

Albert Einstein

STILTSKIN, THE ANGRY IMP

Sad, the miller longs for his daughter's fame.
Sad because on business to the king's court
the miller, who curses his own mediocrity,
lies that his daughter spins gold from straw.

"Oh God," the king exclaims. "Can this be true?
Then show me. Prove it. Bring the girl to me.
Give her a room, a spinning wheel, firelight.
Let the room glitter with gold by morning.

The beautiful daughter turns her profile
to the icy window, waits for daybreak,
believes she will surely be put to death
if she cannot produce gold from straw.

Night is the hunter and finds her
where all hunted animals go, in a corner.
She hunkers down on a stool, ankle deep in straw,
blows breath into her hands to warm them.

The door opens. She thinks she will be slain.
A deformed man, not much higher than her
wooden stool, hobbles in. "Good morrow,
my lass. Why are you crying?"

She tells him of her dilemma with the King,
that she must turn straw into gold by morning.
The dwarf listens, is delighted to bargain

for her necklace. He whirls straw about the room
until it glitters to the floor yellow as butter.

"Someone bring that girl to me," the king shouts.
"If you fill that room again with gold, the prince,
will marry you." She knew she must endure
the dwarf once more. He appears from the winter
night, cold and demanding, owning her heart
in his special way, says that he will, indeed,
transmute straw until it matches the color of the sun.

If I do this deed for you again, you must
give me your first-born child when you are queen.
"Ridiculous," she thought. " I will never be queen.
He will not save me this time." So, she promises
her first child, crouches down on the stool,
waiting for him to fail.

His passionate hands spin commonplace straw
into gold threads bright as fire. The future
queen trembles, slumps because she cannot betray
her promise. The king dies of a sudden stroke.
Now in love, the prince and the girl marry.

She cradles her child in her arms, saunters
into the flower garden, stands among early daffodils.
"I can't give you up," she whispers to her son,
but I promised. There must be another bargain
to nullify my word of honor.

The dwarf arrives to claim the baby. She pleads
for another arrangement. "I'll give you three days
to tell me my name." "Yes. Yes," she cries out.

The dwarf wiggles a fist in her face. "Three days,"
he roars. "You must tell me my name in three days.
Not a minute more."

In a frenzy, she dispatches messengers across the land
who return to her with mouthfuls of names she never heard.
"Surely," she thinks, "the dwarf's name must be among them."

When the little man appears, she is ready to name him.
"Benjamin? Timothy? Jeremiah?" "You have not
named me." He laughs, turns his back to her. She pales,
her heart iced with failure.

Next day, he returns wearing new clothes to celebrate
his conquest. "Bandy-legs, Hunchback, Crooked-shanks."
Such comical names he brushes aside as he does lint
from the cuff of his velvet jacket. "None of them
is my name," he laughs, pulling a handkerchief
from his breast pocket to dab at his smile.

On the third day, a court messenger presents
himself before the queen. "I was climbing a hill
topped by a stand of trees and saw a hut.
Before it, fire burned and a dwarf danced around
the flames, a little man in a velvet suit, hopping
from foot to foot, singing his name again and again
and again." "Can your name be Thomas," she asks the dwarf
the next day. He denies it, stuffs hands into pockets,
paces the floor. "Are you called John?" His hands
touch his face in feigned dismay. " Oh, dear me, no.
I'm afraid not." The dwarf reaches for the baby

just as she decides to end the game.
"Then I shall call you Rumpelstiltskin."
His arms drop to his sides. He sags in defeat,
raises his head and screams, "The Devil told you."
With that, the dwarf sinks into a hole opening in the floor,
waist-deep, tears himself in half, disappears from her life
forever like milkweed fuzz blown to oblivion
by irrefutable gales of wind.

PART SEVEN

A day without laughter is a day wasted.

Charlie Chaplin

PARTY POOCH, 1932

"Howard, dogs are not zoo animals."
Toying with a sandal strap, he answers,
"I call them zoo animals because they dash
away from you like a gazelle or a
galloping giraffe." Howard, a neighbor,
seems obsessed with dog topics lately
because of numerous strays in the vicinity.
We lounge on Aunt Ada's back porch steps,
eating pineapple upside-down cake she just baked.
She and Aunt Liz live next to each other,
and on this steamy, July afternoon perch
across from us on green, outdoor, metal chairs,
waiting for a breeze to cross the patio.

I tell him, "You have the right idea, Howard,
but the wrong species." As if on cue,
a Boston Terrier slinks around the corner
from the alley, halts when it sees people.
The aunts' mouths gape wider than rumble seats,
forksful of cake suspended in mid-air.
They believe any dog that lurks in a yard
other than its own is unquestionably rabid,
so aunts huddle together, pull dresses down
closer to ankles. The dog stares, eyes riveted
to the cake. Uncle Heinie, Aunt Ada's' husband,
ambles out of the house, sees the dog, grabs
a garden hose. "You can't," Howard and I yell
in unison. "The dog isn't rabid. It's not foaming
at the mouth." During the commotion, the terrier,

quick as a cheetah, snatches remaining cake
off the table, tears down the alley out of sight.
Howard and I laugh, and I suspect he is ready
to spout the cliché "Doesn't that take the cake?"
So, I lean toward him, admonish,
"Don't say it, Howard. Don't."

9 788119 654949